Praise for *Trusted*

Trusted: Trust Pillars, Trust Killers, and the Secret to Successful Schools is a powerful and practical read for all educators. As a current school principal, I connected deeply with the real-world experiences and strategies for building trust with staff, students, and families. This book is a must-read for aspiring, current, and veteran school leaders seeking to strengthen relationships and create a culture where trust fuels success at every level!

—**Dr. Rachel Edoho-Eket,** principal, author, speaker, and ASCD faculty member

It's hard to say which of Jen Schwanke's books is my favorite, but *Trusted* has just moved to the top. Offering one of the best historical analyses of U.S. education I've seen, it reminds school leaders that they are not alone—past or present. This book not only identifies trust as a core challenge but also provides practical, real-life strategies for building it with teachers, parents, and students. It should be required reading for anyone committed to leading through trust.

—**William D. Parker,** founder, Principal Matters, LLC

Nothing good happens without trust, and that's what Jen Schwanke has expertly amplified in *Trusted*. Jen has masterfully identified the issues that affect students, educators, school leaders, families, and the community at large. Her unique insights give school leaders tangible ways to establish trust holistically and with a keen eye on societal impact. This book provides the structure for building and sustaining a strong culture where everyone can be seen, heard, and valued. Brava!

—**Dr. Kate Anderson Foley,** CEO, The Education Policy & Practice Group

Trusted

Also by Jen Schwanke

The Principal's Guide to Conflict Management

The Teacher's Principal

The Principal Reboot

You're the Principal! Now What?

Trusted

Trust Pillars Trust Killers and the Secret to Successful Schools

Jen Schwanke

ascd
Arlington, Virginia USA

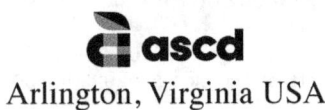

2111 Wilson Boulevard, Suite 300 • Arlington, VA 22201 USA
Phone: 800-933-2723 or 703-578-9600
Website: www.ascd.org • Email: member@ascd.org
Author guidelines: www.ascd.org/write

Richard Culatta, *Chief Executive Officer;* Anthony Rebora, *Chief Content Officer;* Genny Ostertag, *Managing Director, Book Acquisitions & Editing;* Stephanie Bize, *Acquisitions Editor;* Mary Beth Nielsen, *Director, Book Editing;* Katie Martin, *Senior Editor;* Catherine Gillespie, *Graphic Designer;* Cynthia Stock, *Typesetter;* Kelly Marshall, *Production Manager;* Shajuan Martin, *E-Publishing Specialist*

Copyright © 2025 ASCD. All rights reserved. It is illegal to reproduce copies of this work in print or electronic format (including reproductions displayed on a secure intranet or stored in a retrieval system or other electronic storage device from which copies can be made or displayed) without the prior written permission of the publisher. By purchasing only authorized electronic or print editions and not participating in or encouraging piracy of copyrighted materials, you support the rights of authors and publishers. Readers who wish to reproduce or republish excerpts of this work in print or electronic format may do so for a small fee by contacting the Copyright Clearance Center (CCC), 222 Rosewood Dr., Danvers, MA 01923, USA (phone: 978-750-8400; fax: 978-646-8600; web: www.copyright.com). To inquire about site licensing options or any other reuse, contact ASCD Permissions at www.ascd.org/permissions or permissions@ascd.org. For a list of vendors authorized to license ASCD ebooks to institutions, see www.ascd.org/epubs. Send translation inquiries to translations@ascd.org.

ASCD® is a registered trademark of Association for Supervision and Curriculum Development. All other trademarks contained in this book are the property of, and reserved by, their respective owners, and are used for editorial and informational purposes only. No such use should be construed to imply sponsorship or endorsement of the book by the respective owners.

All web links in this book are correct as of the publication date below but may have become inactive or otherwise modified since that time. If you notice a deactivated or changed link, please email books@ascd.org with the words "Link Update" in the subject line. In your message, please specify the web link, the book title, and the page number on which the link appears.

PAPERBACK ISBN: 978-1-4166-3379-2   ASCD product #125016   n8/25
PDF EBOOK ISBN: 978-1-4166-3380-8; see Books in Print for other formats.
Quantity discounts are available: email programteam@ascd.org or call 800-933-2723, ext. 5773, or 703-575-5773. For desk copies, go to www.ascd.org/deskcopy.

Library of Congress Cataloging-in-Publication Data

Names: Schwanke, Jen author
Title: Trusted : trust pillars, trust killers, and the secret to successful schools / Jen Schwanke.
Description: Arlington, VA : ASCD, [2025] | Includes bibliographical references and index.
Identifiers: LCCN 2025015549 (print) | LCCN 2025015550 (ebook) | ISBN 9781416633792 paperback | ISBN 9781416633808 pdf
Subjects: LCSH: Educational leadership—United States | School principals--Professional relationships—United States | Trust—United States
Classification: LCC LB2805 .S444 2025 (print) | LCC LB2805 (ebook) | DDC 371.2/070973—dc23/eng/20250613
LC record available at https://lccn.loc.gov/2025015549
LC ebook record available at https://lccn.loc.gov/2025015550

34 33 32 31 30 29 28 27 26 25   1 2 3 4 5 6 7 8 9 10 11 12

Trusted

1. Trust in Schools: Why It Is Broken and How to Get It Back 1
2. Trustworthy and "Trust Willing" 25
3. Trust Pillars and Trust Killers 45
4. Trust with Teachers 66
5. Trust with Parents 94
6. Trust with Students 116
7. Self-Trust and Beyond 137

Acknowledgments 149

References 150

Index 155

About the Author 163

Trust in Schools:
Why It Is Broken and How to Get It Back

Not long ago, I took a phone call from a principal who was almost speechless with incredulity. "I thought I'd heard it all," she said, "but after the conversation I just had with one of my student's parents, I've been proven wrong!"

She gave me the run-down. A student in her school had been spotted using his phone during a Spanish test. When questioned by the teacher, he admitted he had enlisted a friend to text him answers. So the principal called the student's mother, explaining there were two issues to discuss. The first was the student using his phone during the test, which was a violation of the school's cell phone policy. The second was the cheating.

From the moment she picked up, the mother was defending her son. During a quick call home to brief her on the situation, he'd managed to convince her that his choices were justified. "He *had* to cheat!" the mother shouted at the principal. "The teacher didn't cover the material well enough!" She went on a profane and personal tirade about the teacher, who happened to be one of the school's strongest, most knowledgeable, and most passionate staff members.

The principal responded calmly but firmly. The teacher had covered the material thoroughly, she explained, and if the student had been confused, he had had many opportunities to get help ahead of the test. The principal explained that as a consequence of the cheating, the student would have to retake an alternate test. Further, the principal explained, the student would have his phone confiscated during school hours—a consequence for violating the school's phone use policy.

The mother cursed, called the teacher a bully, threatened a lawsuit, and raged about the "overreaching" of the school staff. Then she turned on the principal. "This is why you have a terrible reputation in this community," she snapped. "You always take the teacher's side. You never fight for kids. No one respects you. No one likes you. I'm just the only one with courage enough to say it." The principal wisely indicated she would end the conversation unless it could proceed as a civil one. The parent hung up.

As the principal recounted the story to me, her voice quavered. "I didn't sign up for this," she said, breaking into sobs. "I don't deserve to be treated this way."

I let her cry, reassuring her she was correct. No, she did not deserve to be treated this way.

"When did it become *us* versus *them*?" she asked. "We are doing such good things at this school. None of her accusations are even remotely true. What happened to trust?"

What Happened to Trust? Exploring Cause, Assigning Blame

Well, a lot has happened to trust. In general, our society has become a place of doubt and skepticism. Fear and anxiety have spiked, and the connectivity that technology enables has, ironically, contributed to diminished connections among people. And educators find themselves in the crosshairs.

Schools always reflect the social and cultural needs, norms, and function of a society. If a society is in a place of uncertainty and distrust, so, too, will be her schools. When a nation experiences loss and change, so, too, do her schools. Political divisiveness, restlessness, and anxiety settles into the fiber of everyday life and threatens our sense of cultural, political, or societal safety. That's when all eyes turn to the schools: *Let's all focus on the coming generation as a way to fix societal ills. Let's look to the children—and look at the people who are working with them.*

One doesn't need to go back far in history to see a correlation between a society's stability and how it treats its educators. Over the years, parents and lawmakers—seeking hope and order—have repeatedly pressured schools to conform to their vision of the future. This pressure creates divided perspectives and conflict between educators and people who think they know what it's like to be an educator. School districts, their superintendents, and their principals, all of whom are trying to protect their teachers and students from the worst of the discontent, become targets. Their efforts at protection can create pressure and an overwhelming workload for these educators—yet that spotlight stays firmly on them, with every move judged and criticized.

What's worse, the criticism often comes with inaccurate or inflamed information gleaned from social media or groups of like-minded people, entrenched in their opinionated echo chambers. Complicated political environments have given rise to many parents questioning their children's school experiences and the "right" that schools have to educate a child. Feeling under attack, educators understandably become defensive and exhausted. For their part, students see their teachers and principals—people they generally respect and admire—become the recipients of mistreatment, arguments, unverified facts, and accusations. When such treatment comes from a child's own parents, whom they also respect and admire, it creates a confusing and misaligned perspective about whom to trust. This all plays out in living rooms, at dinner tables, in school offices, over phone calls, and, unfortunately and damagingly, on social media and partisan media outlets. It feels like a top spinning out of control and further fracturing trust between schools and their communities.

When I work with educators who are grappling with this phenomenon's effect on their professional satisfaction and career goals,

I find it helps to dig into the larger forces behind it. During my doctoral studies of the history of public education in the United States, I learned a great deal about the precarious trust between schools and community. I can therefore assure these educators that all this scrutiny and criticism is an established pattern in U.S. history. When society feels unstable, schools become a target.

Schooling in the United States was established early in the 17th century to teach religious values and academics, particularly reading, which was a skill necessary for children to be able to read the Bible (Chen, 2022). Schools were overseen and developed by committees of local residents (Edwards, 2006). These community members were reluctant to appoint leaders for their schools—superintendents or principals—because of the "strong anti-executive tradition" the colonists held (Brunner et al., 2002). Instead, they relied on clerks who assisted boards of education with typical activities related to schools (Tyack & Hansot, 1982). The reluctance to appoint superintendents slowly began to change with the Land Ordinance of 1786 (Knepper, 2002). The survey highlighted a commitment to education as one of the new country's core values, as the Ordinance dictated townships be divided into 36 sections of 640 acres, with the 16th lot of every township reserved for public schools (Dotson, n.d.). In the end, the federal government allotted more than 145 million acres of public land for public schools. This scope created an undeniable need for a state superintendent to oversee the use of the land, financial transactions, building of schools, hiring of teachers, and enrollment of students (Glass & Franceschini, 2007).

With land, revenue, and superintendents in place, a public system of education emerged. Based on the "common school" movement led by Horace Mann, the system relied on state oversight but also remained committed to local leadership and control. It was created, funded, and supported by educated citizens and open to students who—it was hoped—would grow into educated community members, just like the system's founders. Notably, the system was one "that would discourage participation by females, working and lower-class people, and members of racial minority groups" (Fowler, 2013, p. 32).

In the mid-nineteenth century, 80 percent of Americans lived in rural areas (Tyack & Hansot, 1982). The first common schools were small, one-room buildings with just one teacher. In urban areas, where there were more students to educate, male schoolmasters taught older students in one room upstairs while "woman assistants" taught younger children in another room downstairs (Blount, 1998, p. 27). Common schools lacked organized oversight, but without the restraints of bureaucracy, teachers had full autonomy over how and what they taught, perhaps the only benefit for those who wished to be teachers, as they were poorly paid and poorly trained. Teaching was not acknowledged as a respected profession, so turnover was high—especially for women, who were expected to leave teaching once they married (Blount, 1998).

As the organizational system of schools evolved, male administrators, referred to as "principal teachers," were hired to "monitor female teachers and keep them from getting out of line" (Blount, 1998, p. 26). They also administered exams, evaluated teachers, managed discipline, and visited schools "to observe teachers at work and to assess the quality of student recitations" (p. 27).

Moving into the 20th century, the structure was in place for the education system we know today. But as the nation grappled with societal challenges, trust in schools was tested. Let's take a look at U.S. education over time. It will be eye-opening to see how many of today's challenges have been faced by the leaders who came before us and to count the times in our past when trust in schools has been questioned, challenged, or broken.

1900–1920: Disparities and school boards

The dawn of the 20th century was relatively quiet for the United States, which was focused on managing its growth and establishing its place in the world. Schools, too, were reinforcing the structures to manage growth and handle increased community expectations. There were huge discrepancies in wealth and opportunity among rural, suburban, and urban communities, and these discrepancies were reflected in the nation's schools. There was also a continued divide between the industrializing North and the "stagnant, poor, and rural" South (Verdugo, 2018, p. lix). These disparities caused unrest and anger from parents, who pointed out that children had a different educational experience based on where they lived—a problem that has risen repeatedly over the past century.

Further disparities came from inefficient and politicized school boards, some so large they could not effectively lead. For example, in 1905, Philadelphia had 43 school boards with a total of 559 members. Sixteen cities with populations over 100,000 had boards of 20 members or more. Minneapolis had seven board members, while Hartford, one-third the size of Minneapolis, had 39 board members and committeemen. Every district, every state, and every community conducted school board operations differently, in large part because local control remained a priority (Kirst, 1994). Over time, weary from internal politics and the difficulty of achieving consensus, school boards began considering input from business professionals, who emphasized "centralization, expertise, professionalization, nonpolitical control, and efficiency" (p. 1). Finally, led by the National Education Association (NEA), which was then primarily an organization of school administrators, school board structures were adjusted to become a small, elected group of local leaders. The change, adopted across the country, "purged . . . all connections with political parties and officials of general government, such as mayors and councilmen" (Kirst, 1994, p. 1). Note that recent school board elections across the United States seem to be growing more partisan, threatening to reverse measures enacted more than 100 years earlier.

Smaller boards did not alleviate the pressure on school administrators, who, overwhelmed and overworked, were struggling to handle the vast management tasks they were required to complete. Their responsibilities had grown to include oversight of instructional pedagogy, curricular decisions, and assimilating students into the U.S. culture by providing uniform, standardized subjects and courses (Kowalski, 2005). The interrelated curriculum included reading, spelling, literature, language, writing, history, geography, nature study, kindergarten, normal training, drawing, and numbers (Maxwell, 1904).

When the United States entered World War I, school officials grappled with their role supporting a country at war and managing their community's response to international conflict. In general, those with formal education tended to favor the war, while those with less education were more likely to oppose it. Because patriotism was such an important aspect of curriculum at the time, school officials supported war efforts, yet there was great resistance from many subgroups, primarily women, working-class people, and those in rural areas. The war also brought enormous disruption to the lives of children. Many male students ages 16 and older enlisted, and other students organized ways to support the war effort. Classroom instruction shifted to cover military training and strategy. Students and educators were also affected by rationing and by the absence and deaths of friends and family members (Conway, 2013).

1920–1940: Growing enrollment, a curricular shift, and new politicization

Throughout the 1920s and 1930s, although the United States was still largely rural, the economy began to move away from agriculture and toward industry (Tyack & Hansot, 1982). This shift in the labor market reduced the need for underaged workers, leading to new child labor restrictions. Compulsory attendance laws were enacted, contributing to a growing belief that children should receive formal education for a longer period—through high school—to get a better job and have a more financially secure future. Since 1916, nearly every state had required students between the ages of 6 and 17 to attend school. Sharp increases in enrollment were felt acutely at the high school level; between 1890 and 1920, new high schools opened at the rate of one per day (Lepore, 2022). In 1920, 83.2 percent of children between the ages 5 and 17 were enrolled in school; by 1940, it was 94.2 percent (Tyack et al., 1984).

A curricular shift also took place, particularly in urban areas, as schools offered a more utilitarian and vocational education for skilled trades. Cost management and efficiency were incorporated into educational decision making, pressuring administrators to run their schools like businesses (Glass & Franceschini, 2007). Due to limited funding and resources, superintendents were forced to engage more directly in legislation and politics (Kowalski, 2005). This remains true today, often creating similar issues of trust between those doing the work (teachers and principals) and those making decisions about how it should be done (legislatures, businesspeople, and top district officials).

The Great Depression

Although many of the United States's troubles during the Great Depression were blamed on the stock market crash on October 24, 1929, the truth is much more sobering. As mentioned earlier, the nation had seen huge disparities in wealth and poverty for years, and much of the educational system, made up of 127,531 districts, was "already in the throes of depression well before the crash" (Tyack et al., 1984, p. 28). Schools experienced inequity in resources, facilities, and impact, spanning a wide spectrum ranging from extreme affluence to shocking poverty. Compared to urban areas, rural areas had almost double the birth rates, lower per-pupil expenditures, lower school attendance rates, and fewer health and social services. With the economy in crisis, many young people were unable to find work, so they enrolled in school. From 1929 to 1934, enrollment of secondary students went from 3,911,000 to 5,669,000, and graduation rates jumped from 26.2 percent to 39.2 percent.

With higher enrollment, communities had an opportunity to have more exposure to the value of education, which could have resulted in greater trust between communities and schools. But economic shortfalls forced boards to slash jobs and services. There were clashes over local control of schools, states asserting their power, federal economic distress, and the impact of powerful private business, "both within the educational system—between liberals and conservatives, teachers and school boards—and in the larger community, over the funding of education and over the ideological ferment the depression created" (Tyack et al., 1984, p. 57). Many boards cut "fads and frills," including health services, physical education, night schools, adult education, kindergarten, and vocational schooling (p. 39). These cuts were painful, as they involved programs that had been a great source of pride to administrators. Tens of thousands of teachers marched against financial decisions, the destruction of the school system, and the devastating impact budget cuts had on teachers and students. Societal crises like this reinforce the cyclical nature of a society's trust in itself and its trust in schools. Precarious finances, fluctuating enrollment, teacher pay, and the input from private industry have continued to be challenges faced by school districts, and they all raise emotion and challenge trust.

Still, in the mid-1900s, regardless of the poverty or wealth of the surrounding community, schools provided crucial community connections. They hosted pie suppers, school picnics, plays, recitals, dances, Christmas celebrations, and ice cream socials. Families came from rural areas to their nearest school to take part and lift community morale. Urban areas transformed their schools into community centers and food service stations. In places where schools managed to stay open—even if staff were working for little or no pay—teachers and students still showed up (Ganzel & Reinhardt, 2003). In other words, trust in the country's education system was being tested, but many still depended on schools to hold communities together.

1940–1960: Social tension

When the United States officially entered World War II in December 1941, there was a swift and enormous demand for labor and troops, which led to a massive exodus of secondary students leaving school to go to work or the armed services (Tyack et al., 1984). At home without their husbands and older sons or brothers, mothers and children lived in fear of bomb attacks and watched the emergence of deep racism against Japanese people and Japanese Americans. In school, children and teachers shared in the feeling of danger with mandated air raid drills and blackouts. Students were marched to basements or asked to crouch beneath their desks, perpetuating even more fear (Tuttle, 1993, pp. 5–6). These scenarios echo the fear and debate we have recently faced with school safety and pandemic protocol, when arguments about "what is best for the children" cause deep divides and put teachers in the middle of bitter disagreements.

Meanwhile, the nation's long-standing tendency to segregate students by class was becoming a topic of deep concern for social scientists and community members. Firmly entrenched cultural norms separated students of means from students living in poverty. Poor students tended to take a vocational track of classes, while more affluent ones took an academic and college preparatory track. Discipline decisions were vastly disparate, with poorer students given harsh consequences and wealthy students given a pass. Grades were correlated with a family's wealth. In all ways, it seemed, the two classes operated in distinctly separate worlds (Tyack et al., 1984).

Educators avoided discussing these problems. Aubrey Williams, a social and civil rights activist through the years of the Depression and World War II, said to the New York United Parents Association, "I often wonder why educators do not spend more of their time discussing the great spread of family income" (Tyack et al., 1984, p. 171). Perhaps they did not know what to do about such a troubling problem. Sadly, much of this problem remains today, and it is still rarely discussed in open, honest dialogue. In some states, school funding models perpetuate these disparities year after year, working under complex funding structures that are confusing and nonsensical for taxpayers. Again, under these circumstances, it is no wonder there is a lack of trust between communities and schools.

Still, schools found their footing for a short time after 1945, when the war ended and administrators enjoyed a temporary peace. Had they had a crystal ball, though, they would have known to prepare for the storm of social unrest that would ultimately lead to a civil rights battle, a mandate to desegregate districts in response to a pivotal Supreme Court case, and a wave of case law decisions that would change how districts viewed students and honored their rights.

The U.S. Supreme Court, Black educators, and early consolidation

On May 17, 1954, the U.S. Supreme Court ruled in the seminal *Brown v. Board of Education* case. Districts were to desegregate "with all deliberate speed," reflecting the Court's hopes to dismantle a long and painful chapter of racial segregation in America's education system. It was the first time the Court had made such a wide-reaching decision about public schools and the first time such a vast number of

Americans voiced their opinions about public education (Simmons, 2005, p. 254). Post-*Brown* integration efforts were disastrous for Black educators, highly talented and well-trained, who had chosen the profession because it was one of the only well-respected career options for Black people (Fultz, 2004; Lutz, 2017; Rousmaniere, 2013). Although Black educators had long been diminished in the profession, making 60 percent less than their white counterparts, the desegregation order kicked off an entirely new sort of racism when districts complied with the desegregation order by simply closing Black schools and cutting, demoting, or firing Black educators (Rousmaniere, 2013). Before 1954, there were roughly 82,000 Black educators. After *Brown,* tens of thousands of Black educators lost their jobs (Lutz, 2017). The number of Black principals fell by 90 percent, approaching "literal extinction" (Rousmaniere, 2013, p. 113). In the South alone, 38,000 Black teachers lost their jobs, often in the form of demotions or re-assignments in which they were given jobs outside their qualification area and then fired for incompetence (Lutz, 2017).

Meanwhile, though some districts began *Brown*-mandated compliance efforts, others refused to integrate. Organizations such as the National Association for the Advancement of Colored People, the Black Panther Party, and the Southern Christian Leadership Conference protested, fighting for equal opportunities and representation within their communities and their country (Simmons, 2005). The civil rights movement was born. It was televised and watched across America, which pressured school districts to change the racial diversity of school leaders and teachers. Counterprotests by groups such as the Ku Klux Klan and White Citizens Councils fought segregation alongside other uprisings resisting social change—antifeminists protested women's rights, and fundamentalists banded together for restoration of traditional religious and patriotic approaches, including reinforcing the Bible as a foundational guide and attempting to bring prayer back to classrooms (Tyack & Hansot, 1982).

Educational leaders wanted calm, orderly procedures that followed protocol. Yet, suddenly, they found themselves in the crosshairs of conflicting pressures from communities and were unprepared and unaccustomed to protests, confrontations, riots, sit-ins, boycotts, and ongoing legal challenges (Tyack & Hansot, 1982). Then, adding to the pressure, the U.S. Office of Education passed the Elementary and Secondary Education Act of 1965, which threatened to withhold federal funding from districts that refused to comply with requirements to desegregate (Tyack & Hansot, 1982).

Ongoing school consolidation

In 1959, James Conant published a book titled *The American High School Today*, which came to be known as "The Conant Report" (Conant, 1959). Conant had never worked in a public high school, nor had he served as an administrator in a K–12 setting. He was a university scholar and war hero, which contributed to his professional prominence and made the book a bestseller. It was read and quoted by hundreds of thousands of Americans, including school boards, parents, teachers, and administrators. Although many disputable claims were made in the report, many districts responded to the book's allegations by implementing widespread changes that were later likened to "a national disaster" with "tragic" consequences for the nation's students (Koerner, 1960, p. 1). Specifically, Conant's recommendations called upon schools to group students by ability and prioritize the education of those identified as highly intelligent and "academically inclined" (Durham, 1959. p. 179). He also took issue with the number of schools that served small communities and pushed back against local control of schools. He declared that any high school with a graduating class of less than 100 was too small to provide an appropriately diverse curriculum (Kowalski, 2003, p. 13).

Consolidating schools was controversial, especially in rural areas. Again, protests and anger bubbled up. Parents felt betrayed by the entire system, especially when their protests failed to stop consolidation (Kowalski, 2003). Between 1930 and 1980, a full 90 percent of school districts were eliminated (Knezevich, 1984).

The push toward consolidation, initially borne from Conant's academic philosophy, had morphed into one of efficiency and space. With state and local funding reduced to encourage consolidation, districts were forced to cut teaching staff, eliminate programs, and consolidate buildings. Communities balked at passing bond levies or increasing taxes, limiting community funds. At the same time, the cost of running a district was rising. Federal mandates were passed for special education students with no allocation of funds to help implement the changes. With fewer new teachers being hired, the cost of salaries rose with the price of paying veteran teachers. Inflation rose. School administrators tried to solve their enrollment and financial challenges by closing schools, then experienced the rage and fury of communities desperate to keep their neighborhood schools open. School closures became "the hottest of political hot potatoes in countless towns, suburbs, and cities" across the country (Tyack et al., 1984, p. 198).

At the same time, organized teacher unions found the power of their collective voices. Teacher walkouts led to an executive order from President John F. Kennedy giving federal employees the right to collectively bargain (Bloch & Karson, 1972; Hannaway & Mittleman, 2011). This was a seismic shift for school districts and school leaders, who now had to work with teachers for "the settlement of salaries and benefits, working conditions, evaluation procedures, transfer policies, assignment policies, and policies for making reductions in force (layoffs) decisions" (George et al., 2018, p. 1). Community members watched closely and had strong, emotional responses—divided between pro-union and anti-union—and their sentiments often tested the trust between a community who either supported its teachers or felt they should not be able to advocate for better work conditions.

Crises of leadership

While schools were undergoing these drastic adjustments, America itself was entering a period that would become the pinnacle of a devastating chapter in the country's history. John F. Kennedy, Malcom X, Martin Luther King Jr., and Robert F. Kennedy were all assassinated within five years. Leading a school district through the loss of so many leaders, all of whom were working to bring peace and nonviolent change to the United States, must have felt like an insurmountable task. In addition, following *Brown*, there were two additional Supreme Court decisions that had enormous impact on public schools. The Court protected student freedom of speech with its 1969 decision on the *Tinker v. Des Moines Independent School District* case and protected students' right to due process with the *Goss v. Lopez* decision in 1975.

Previously reluctant to weigh in on school districts, the U.S. Supreme Court had now outlined mandates and expectations for public school districts on three key issues—desegregation, free speech, and discipline—all of which lessened school system autonomy. Perhaps because of this, school boards and citizens became more critical of the work of administrators, questioning their expertise and insisting on better outcomes and higher expectations. Further, the tumultuous 1970s led to a decline in both the material and emotional benefits of teaching, as startling statistics attest. In 1961, half of American teachers said that if given a chance to be an educator again, they would choose to do so. By the end of the 1970s, only 22 percent answered yes (Tyack et al., 1984).

School administrators also needed to adjust to the "tremendous growth in the specialized functions of the school, including career education, bilingual education, the teaching of nutrition and health, remedial reading, and so on" (Kirst, 1994, p. 1). All these initiatives came with input from outsiders. Heading toward the 1980s, "everyone wanted to run the schools: courts, state legislatures, federal officials, special interest groups, teachers' unions. Everyone wanted to give marching orders, but no one wished to buy the boots" (Tyack et al., 1984, p. 190). Again, trust in schools diminished as educators' work continued to be criticized and micromanaged by outside entities.

1980–2000: More criticism and scrutiny

In 1983, President Ronald Reagan's National Commission on Excellence in Education released *A Nation at Risk: The Imperative for Educational Reform*. For teachers, principals, and school leaders, the report was a scathing critique of their work and a critical call to action. For parents of schoolchildren, the report was a summary of all the ways schools were failing in America. It predicted a nation's downfall, sending ripples of fear and anger through the nation's communities (Hunt & Staton, 1996). Of all things that had broken trust between community and schools, this report may have been the most damaging of all. Many districts came under fire in the media for internal conflict and operational failure, and their boards of education received the brunt of the blame (Kirst, 1994). State legislatures and education agencies challenged boards to consider their conventional approaches and assumptions about school leadership (Björk & Kowalski, 2005). School finance reform became an ongoing discussion, as was pressure on districts to develop ongoing competency assessments and adopt rigorous academic standards. Districts had to focus on adopting national or state learning standards, considering updated policies for their districts, and examining what their students were able to learn and do (Kirst, 1994).

2000–2024: Crisis and conflict

On January 8, 2002, President George W. Bush signed the controversial No Child Left Behind (NCLB) Act into law. It reauthorized the Elementary and Secondary Education Act of 1965 and replaced the Bilingual Education Act of 1968.

NCLB was built on an increase of high-stakes standardized testing and pressured schools to be accountable for the results. There were penalties for districts that did not meet "adequate yearly progress" toward the goals outlined in NCLB. Three years later, the reauthorization of the 1975 Individuals with Disabilities Improvement Act (IDEA) was passed, providing updates and modifications on special education services and protocols for schools (Sass, 2021). These new mandates were unfunded and thus needed to be supported by local and state dollars. The requirements would cause significant increases in staffing, resources, training, and oversight.

Meanwhile, the U.S. economy had entered a recession. States and schools made significant cuts to their budgets. In 2013, 50 public schools in Chicago were closed—the largest mass school closing in U.S. history. Detroit, Philadelphia, and Washington, DC, also closed large numbers of schools, eliminating thousands of jobs (Sass, 2021).

Added to this upheaval was a new and shocking challenge to the sense of safety that had always been enjoyed in schools: school shootings—the first of which, in 1999 at Columbine High School in Colorado, killed 15 people and injured 20 others (History.com Editors, 2009).

And there was more. The emergence of the Common Core State Standards was yet another source of anger, anxiety, and frustration for educators. Drafted in 2009, the Common Core was adopted in 2010 by 40 states and the District of Columbia. In the next two years, five more states joined. Much of the country didn't notice or worry—until 2014, when implementation of the Common Core's accompanying assessments took hold. Suddenly, and with increasing intensity, a nationwide resistance ensued "from an unusual coalition of right-wingers, liberals, teachers, and parents, for a variety of very different reasons" (McArdle, 2014, para. 4). The debates led to vastly different reactions from states, with some threatening to repeal the standards, others rewriting the standards to better fit their state's political environment, and still others fully adopting the standards.

And, yes, there was still more. In early 2020, the COVID-19 pandemic quickly consumed school leaders' attention, requiring them to flip instruction to a remote model, which meant securing and distributing technology, retraining teachers, revamping school lunch programs, setting standards for grading practices, tracking student attendance, keeping morale high while focusing on each student's needs, and communicating with a public that was both critical and anxious.

Already split in opinions about the response to pandemic protocol, the nation experienced a reckoning when, on May 20, 2020, George Floyd was murdered in Minneapolis by a white police officer after a store clerk suspected Floyd was using counterfeit money. Issues of police brutality, racial profiling, and a lack of accountability for law enforcement had been simmering for years, and Floyd's murder, a nine-minute suffocation captured on video, set off a firestorm of anger, grief, and racial tension. Once again, eyes turned to school systems. Many parents and community members demanded action from schools through initiatives that would teach students about diversity, equity, and inclusion. Many others pushed back against such efforts, seeking bans on books, suing for restrictions on LGBTQIA+

protections, and developing stances on concepts such as critical race theory. Social media raged, and media outlets chased stories of political outrage and divided communities. School boards were inundated with pleas, demands, and fury from a spectrum of parents and citizens with opposing beliefs.

As the pandemic waned, schools reeled under the pressure. In the years since, academic data, student discipline, social-emotional learning, safety, and finance all continue to be hot-button issues. What are public schools expected to focus on today? What should be done about the issues that concern us so deeply—school shootings, curricular standards, equality, and equity of access? Unfortunately, these questions have opened administrators to critical and discontented communities, eager to find fault in their school districts. Misinformation and distrust snowball, breaking trust between district officials, principals, teachers, and parents.

In viewing the historical context of discontent in schools, it's not surprising—though it is certainly still unsettling—to find ourselves, once again, grappling with the effects of decisions being made outside our individual school walls. With high political emotion, executive orders, partisan lawmaking, and mandates that flip-flop depending on state and government leadership, it is again a time of anxiety and unpredictability for our schools. For that reason, it is more critical than ever that school leaders prioritize earning the trust of students, staff, and community.

A Summary of Change in Education and Why It Matters

Let's summarize recent changes into a timeline (see Figure 1). The inspiration for this compilation came from Jamie Vollmer in his book *Schools Cannot Do It Alone* (2010), though I have adjusted Vollmer's additional list to reflect my own research and experiences. Please note that some of the rollouts of these initiatives may have occurred at varying paces and to varying degrees, depending on the state, district, and school.

Figure 1. A Capsule History of U.S. Education Initiatives

Era	Initiative
1600s	First public schools appeared • Idea: Basic reading, writing, and arithmetic to support a new society • Originally for white children, with hopes they would be able to read the Bible • Family and churches bore responsibility for raising children
1700s–1800s	• Land Ordinance earmarks land for schools; finances become more complicated • Curriculum expands, adding some civics, science, social studies, and geography
1900s	Industrialization intensifies • Idea: Schools can support society's needs (provide workers for industry) • Sorting of students between "thinkers" (those who stay in school) and "doers" (those who enter the workforce or work in agriculture)
1910s	• Nutrition education • Immunization • Health (Activities in the health arena multiply every year.)
1910s–1930s	• Physical education (including organized athletics) • The practical arts/domestic science/home economics (including sewing and cooking) • Vocational education (including industrial and agricultural education) • Mandated school transportation
1940s	• Business education (including typing, shorthand, and bookkeeping) • Art and music • Speech and drama • Half-day kindergarten • School lunch programs (shifting to schools the job of feeding America's children one-third of their daily meals.)
1950s	• Expanded science and math education • Safety education • Driver's education • Expanded music and art education • Stronger foreign language requirements • Sex education
1960s	• Advanced Placement programs • Head Start • Preschool • Socioeconomic considerations • Adult education • Consumer education (purchasing resources, rights and responsibilities) • Career education (occupational options, entry-level skill requirements) • Peace, leisure, and recreation education

Era	Initiative
1970s	- Drug and alcohol abuse education - Parenting education (techniques and tools for healthy parenting) - Behavior adjustment classes (including classroom and communication skills) - Character education - Special education - Equal opportunity programs (greatly expanded athletic programs for girls) - Environmental education - Women's studies - African American and Indigenous heritage education - School breakfast programs
1980s	- Keyboarding and computer education - Global education - Multicultural education - Nonsexist education - English-as-a-second-language and bilingual education - Teen pregnancy awareness - Hispanic heritage education - Early childhood education - Jump Start, Early Start, Even Start, and Prime Start - Full-day kindergarten - Preschool programs for children at risk - After-school programs for children of working parents - Alternative education in all its forms - "Stranger danger" education - Anti-smoking education - Sexual abuse prevention education - Expanded health and psychological services - Child abuse monitoring (a legal requirement for all teachers)
1990s	- Conflict resolution and peer mediation - HIV/AIDS education - CPR training - Inclusive practices (versus pullout) - Expanded computer and internet education - Distance learning - Tech prep and school-to-work programs - Technical adequacy - Assessment - Post-secondary enrollment options - Concurrent enrollment options - Goals initiatives - Expanded talented and gifted opportunities - At-risk and dropout prevention - Homeless education (including causes and effects on children) - Gang education (urban centers) - Service learning - Bus safety, bicycle safety, gun safety, and water safety education

(continued)

Figure 1. A Capsule History of U.S. Education Initiatives *(continued)*

Era	Initiative
2000s	• Funding wars • Bullying prevention • Anti-harassment policies (gender, race, religion, or national origin) • Expanded early childhood education programs • Elevator and escalator safety instruction • Body mass index evaluation (obesity monitoring) • Organ donor education and awareness programs • Personal financial literacy • Entrepreneurial and innovation skills development • Media literacy development • Contextual learning skill development • Health and wellness programs
2010s–2020s	• Internet usage/responsibility/cyber safety • College/career readiness enhancement • Increased literacy demands in the youngest learners • Loss of play/increase of standardized testing • Email, texting, videoconference etiquette • Counseling for mental health awareness (including suicide prevention) • Health and wellness • Increased drug/alcohol/vaping training and awareness programs • Code and policy for off-campus activities (discipline) • Lockdown/ALICE training/active shooter responses • Entrepreneurial and innovation skills development • Credit recovery programs • Online learning programs • College credit programs • Common Core • STEM • Response to intervention (RTI) • Multitiered systems of support (MTSS) • Health and wellness programs • "Portrait of a Graduate" goals • Positive behavioral interventions and supports (PBIS) • Technology instruction and 1:1 implementation • Expanded early childhood care/education • Resurgence of technical skills • Increased testing and accountability • National "test site" mandates • Increased training for educators • LGBTQIA+ litigation and appeal • NIL (name, image, and likeness) laws for athletes • Parent rights and privacy laws

I occasionally show this list to principal groups, and I can hear an audible "Ohhh" as they process how many new initiatives have been added to their plates—and how few things have come *off*. Seeing this list is validating; it's no wonder we feel worn thin! Students, parents, and community members all come to us with their own needs and expectations, which we strive to recognize and meet. But directives from federal laws, state legislators, courts, and local district leadership have all increased in intensity, making for a very heavy load indeed. And from a principal's perspective, it can feel impossible to manage so many mandates at once.

Another reason I wanted to spend time on this long history lesson is to call attention to how the ups and downs of a society affect its schools. When I feel overwhelmed with a community's criticisms, it comforts me to remember that top leadership jobs in school districts have always been difficult, dating back to the creation of the first organized schools. The community has always been critical and quick to anger. National politics have always directly impacted the work of school districts. The pressure has always been intense, and it always will be.

I have come to believe the only way to be successful as a school leader is to learn to ride the inevitable ups and downs. Said differently, if school officials hope for a time of quiet and calm, or if we believe we can solve all the problems we face, we will never feel successful. The trick is to accept the job as the one that it has always been and will always be, full of challenge, emotion, and conflict. There is only one thing school leaders can count on: the predictability of unpredictability.

Now, the good news: when leaders accept the natural ebb and flow of conflict, and when we understand society's impact on our schools, we can redirect our energy to aspects of the job where we can make a very real and positive difference. One of these is building trust.

Trust Defined

Trust is difficult to define without getting into complicated nuances about emotions. Even so, we all know how it feels to trust someone, and we know how it feels to be trusted by others. As Simon Sinek

(2021) has said, "Trust is like love. Both parties have to feel it before it really exists."

For the purposes of this book, let's think of trust as an ideal. If I were writing a school culture statement, it would read like this: *A culture of trust in a school means each student, staff member, and community member feels valued, respected, safe, and able to grow into the best versions of themselves.*

As educators, we can readily acknowledge the difficulty in obtaining this ideal, especially when schools are under such scrutiny. Yet it helps to remember there *are* very high levels of trust in many schools and with the communities they serve. In these schools, trust has become its own culture, and the conduits to it are the teachers. Consider: there are more than 93 million teachers in the world, according to the International Task Force on Teachers for Education (2019). Most of these teachers have earned the trust of their students and community. In a recent survey done in the district of one of my colleagues, parents indicated higher levels of trust in their children's teachers than in the school's administrators. Research tells us that the trust in teachers, by teachers, and *between* teachers has a direct impact on a school's openness and the health of the school climate (Tschannen-Moran & Hoy, 1998).

It shouldn't come as a surprise that the most trusted people in a school environment are often teachers. They are the ones most likely to connect with students and know and talk with parents. Further, their relationship with students is based on a well-understood arrangement: the teacher is trusted to teach academic content while making a child feel successful in learning said content. In her work examining trust in educational environments, Victoria E. Barlow (2001) points out that trust is actually a judgment. We judge whether someone or something that we are relying on "will perform as expected and will not fail." This judgment is an interactive process between the person judging and the person being judged. Barlow continues: "This means that the disposition, needs, and capacities of the individual making the judgment are an essential part of the equation, and that trust cannot be determined by the qualities of the object of trust alone" (p. 8). In other words, in an educational environment, there is no specific set of personality traits or character attributes that ensure others will trust us; it's the relationship and experiences among people that create or diminish trust. I've seen students have deep, unwavering trust in teachers who are kind, gentle, and loving, and I've seen the exact same trust for teachers who are tough, brusque, and unemotional. There is no set way to *be* or mindset to have that guarantees a teacher will be trusted. This leads us to the key point of this book: it is our relationships with one another that allow us to build—and enjoy!—the resulting culture of trust in our schools.

Visualizing a Culture of Trust

Let's take a moment to talk about what a culture of trust might look and feel like in an ideal setting.

Principals
- Are honest, straightforward, and empathetic to the unique challenges of each student, teacher, and parent.
- Do not need to micromanage others.
- Empower others to take leadership roles and express authentic gratitude for a job well done.
- Communicate often and with care.
- Guard staff privacy and avoid gossiping about others.
- Remember the ever-changing challenges of being a classroom teacher.
- Connect well with parents and appreciate parents' instinctual defense of their children.
- Develop strong rapport with students as individuals and as part of the larger student body.
- Make difficult decisions to protect students and teachers from harm.

Teachers
- Are willing to "own" their responsibilities.
- Give and take in equal measure.
- Offer students empathy and grace.

- Maintain a classroom environment in which expectations are both high and attainable.
- Accept and give feedback in a respectful way.
- Understand that they are part of a team and find ways to contribute to the greater good.
- Take pride in the work of the school and stay connected to their purpose.
- Respond to challenges from students with respectful and professional interaction.

Students

- Are aware of their school's vision and mission and take responsibility for contributing to a positive school culture.
- Take opportunities to rectify their mistakes and improve.
- Understand they can discuss problems with their teachers, counselors, and, if necessary, the principal.
- Hold one another accountable for meeting high expectations and upholding community standards.
- Capitalize on leadership opportunities and accept support when leading others.
- Apply themselves when pursuing goals.
- Get to know their teachers and peers and enjoy opportunities to interact.
- Respect the perspectives of others.

Although the behaviors I've listed provide a foundation for symbiotic trust, it's also true that trust cannot be measured with a simple checklist. When hundreds or even thousands of people—many of them students, young and still developing into the people they will someday be—are together in a small space, trust can be challenged or broken easily. But trust can also be repaired. What role might principals take in creating, modeling, and articulating components of trust? In the next chapter, we will dive into the reciprocal nature of trust by considering how to be both *trustworthy* and *"trust willing."*

Trustworthy and "Trust Willing"

Chapter 1's deep dive into history highlighted how society tends to project its uneasiness onto schools. For school administrators, this means living in a state of anxiousness; many of us go about our work waiting for the next emergency, the next negative incident, the next round of backlash. Although most times the situation is not of our doing, we are still required to address it, and it's expected that our fix will satisfy everyone involved or affected.

Being in reactive mode is exhausting. Administrators would much rather be proactive in how we lead our schools, as we know how much more effective it is to get in front of problems rather than fix them when they arise. Yet being an educational leader often requires us to lead from behind—hearing about a negative incident, unraveling the details of the problem, and making a plan to clean it up.

It's also worth pointing out another common frustration of being an educator: most non-educators feel confident that they understand what it takes to run a school and a classroom. After all, everyone was once a student, so they have their own experiences to draw upon, right? I often hear non-educators—parents, community members, stakeholder groups, board of education members—say things like, "When I was in school...." and "Why don't you just...." and "We need to go back to...." Remarks like this may be intended to offer perspective or advice, but what they more often do is close the door on productive conversation.

During the height of the COVID-19 pandemic, for example, a parent called me in frustration because her children were struggling to navigate the online learning management system. "Can't you just make a bunch of copies of worksheets and mail them out to all of us?" she asked. "That worked perfectly well for me when I was a student." I tried to explain how efficient, effective, timely, and financially responsible it was to house resources in the virtual classroom, but she refused to listen. For over a year, long after her children had settled into a successful online learning rhythm, she remained angry. I saw her in the grocery store not long ago, and even then, years after our first conversation about worksheets, she took the chance to comment on how technology was ruining education. There was—there is—no chance of changing her mind.

I understand the appeal of "the good old days." Yet I also know that every classroom, and every child, has a unique path and that the world truly *is* different today than it was yesterday. When parents (or other non-educators) project their own school experience onto the current reality, it does more than communicate distrust of the professional educator's expertise; it also discounts societal change. Schools do still focus on the fundamentals of reading, writing, and math, but they are also responsible for much more: sciences, art, social studies, social emotional instruction, AI use, digital literacy, content integration, hands-on learning, project-based units, financial literacy, college and career preparation, and so on. We can't make the mistake of looking to decades-old school experiences as a way to judge *current* educational environments.

Trying to explain that a complex world requires a complex educational approach is an argument lost on many people. And the conversation is impossible to resolve because both sides are wary of the other's perspective. Unfortunately, the divide between educators in the field and the people who are watching from outside continues to grow, deepening distrust between school and the communities we serve.

A similar trust divide can exist within a school, too, among active educators who are working side-by-side toward the same goals. It can live between teachers and their principal and between staff members themselves. When I was a teacher, there were colleagues I was hesitant to trust, and I know there were colleagues who didn't trust me. I was younger then, and, regretfully, I participated in unhealthy and damaging behavioral patterns that undermined trust, such as gossip and cliques. Later, when I first got a job as a principal, I started to think more carefully about trust and my role in it. It was deeply important to me that the staff trust me, so I poured all my energy into being the kind of leader my staff would trust. Whenever I concluded I had not built—or preserved—a sense of trust with a teacher, staff member, or colleague, I felt like a failure. Interestingly, although I prioritized being trustworthy, it never occurred to me to think about my openness to trusting others. In the beginning, I was instinctively cautious about my interactions with parents, students, and teachers. I was often cynical about their motives and actions. I was working on trust as if it were just a one-way street. *I want people to trust me,* I thought. I never thought, *I want to trust them, too.*

Trust is interactive. It is an ongoing cycle—trust feeds trust. Principals are aware that they are constantly being judged, but it's worth admitting that we, too, are always judging others—intentionally or not—to determine whether they deserve *our* trust. We evaluate how they treat their students, the way they interact with parents, and how dedicated they are to the school. We trust parents when they stay in their lane and let us do our work, offering support and understanding when things get complicated with their children. We trust students when they follow school norms and don't hurt one another. Of course, these components are constantly being challenged, which can make principals increasingly cautious about where they place their trust. It can be confusing to *want* to trust someone but know, or feel, that we *can't.*

Research by Maister and colleagues (2001) tells us most professionals find workplace trust to be a complicated issue. Trust is a concept often applied to close personal relationships, even though its value in a professional setting is indisputable. However, at work, we can't necessarily count on the reciprocity of trust. We can't know for sure if we are trusted in the same way that we trust. It's like trying to achieve a perfect balance on a teeter-totter, with no one giving or taking more than the other person. When I feel off-balance in relation to trust, it's usually because one end of the teeter-totter has risen or plunged. In other words, trust is interactional and reciprocal, and whether passive or deliberate, its effects "belong" to the people who participate in the interaction.

In his bestselling book, *The Five Dysfunctions of a Team,* Patrick Lencioni (2002) uses a pyramid-style graphic to outline what makes effective teams. Trust is the base, the foundation that supports everything else. Without trust, a team falls into disarray and becomes unproductive. Absence of trust is a dysfunction Lencioni describes as an "unwillingness to be vulnerable within the group . . . not genuinely open with one another about their mistakes and weaknesses" (p. 188). Without vulnerability, openness, and acknowledgment of weakness, a functional team becomes an impossibility. Without trust as a foundation, team members fear conflict, resist commitment, avoid accountability, and become inattentive to results.

Lencioni (2002) also untangles the ways we overuse—and misuse—the word *trust*. Typically, we think of trust as our ability to use past experiences to predict and understand a person's behavior. Yet trust in a workplace also involves the ability and willingness to be vulnerable, to have "confidence among team members that their peers' intentions are good, and that there is no reason to be protective or careful around the group" (p. 195). Being vulnerable is difficult in many workplaces, especially those in which competitiveness is rewarded. To have a culture in which colleagues are pitted against one another in career advancement and education is costly; distrustful work environments lead to drops in energy as everyone "manages" their behavior. Morale is low, meetings are dreaded, risks are avoided. When we don't feel trusted or don't trust those with whom we work, we conceal our mistakes, avoid asking for help, jump to conclusions, hold grudges, and avoid being with our colleagues.

Why Trust Matters in Schools

Principals are the instructional leaders of their buildings. Supporting the academic rigor, student achievement, and overall student growth is a principal's primary role. However, instructional leadership is just part of school leadership, one aspect of the principal's greater mission, which is to cultivate the well-being of teachers and students and produce positive learning outcomes. Throughout this book, I will remind you of this purpose by pointing out the tie between trust and results and by reflecting on the role of trust in the overall scope of instructional leadership. By way of example, we might ask, "How does a principal's trust-building behaviors affect instruction?" In a systematic review and meta-analysis of research, we find direct relational evidence between principals' trust behaviors and student outcomes (Liebowitz & Porter, 2019). That's the most important reason trust matters in a school setting—because it helps students learn and grow.

> *Principals who work toward trusting relationships with their school communities will positively impact instruction, academic achievement, and student growth.*

Knowing this, let's discuss two essential components of trust. The first is the most familiar: others' ability to trust us. Being a trustworthy educator involves being honest, transparent, and following through on promises. The manifestations of this are felt in our schools when others think of us as *trustworthy*. As mentioned above, though, there is another, less discussed component of trust that eludes many principals. It's the ability and willingness to trust others. Part of being *trust willing* is allowing faculty and staff to do their work without questioning, changing, "fixing," or criticizing their output.

Let's take a closer look at both administrator trustworthiness and trust willingness, starting with the importance of others trusting us.

Being Trustworthy

Because everyone thinks they know how schools should work, we administrators face accountability pressure from many stakeholders. The pressure feels more intense if there is an absence of trust from colleagues within the building. Let's start there.

Some teachers, students, and parents are, quite simply, predisposed to distrust their principal. As we learned in Chapter 1, the first schools were set up with an expressly anti-executive mindset—the goal was to *not* have someone in charge of the schools. The first public schools were managed by the teacher and a council made up of community members. From the very first school, a principal figure was considered a bad thing. Later, when it became obvious that schools did need a leader, and roles such as *principal, headmaster,* and *superintendent* were developed, there was a hesitation about fully trusting and accepting these people as leaders. Even though hundreds of years have passed, this mindset has never completely gone away. It's an anti-executive mindset that is present in many industries, perpetuated and complicated by organized labor movements, necessary legal challenges and protections, and misaligned goals: no one trusts the boss, and the boss doesn't trust anyone.

It helps principals to recognize this pre-existing distrust, because if they make the mistake of assuming they will be trusted simply because they were hired to be in charge of things, it can be a confusing mess to untangle. A new principal once said to me, "Every day, I feel a negative, cautious distance from my school community. I don't understand this! I haven't been in the school long enough to give them reason to distrust me." It was a valid point. Why do people hesitate to trust us when we've done nothing untrustworthy?

When I work with principals like this one, or with any school leader who is struggling to establish or maintain trusting relationships within their building, I remind them of a pattern I've identified over the years. First, about a quarter of the people are going to like and trust you no matter what you do, because you are the boss and that's how they think about bosses. Another quarter of the people are going to dislike and distrust you no matter what you do for the exact same reason: because you're the boss and that's how they think about bosses. The remaining half of your people will waffle back and forth, depending on your school's culture, personal things about you, and how much they believe in your leadership. Explaining this breakdown homes in on a razor-thin distinction between the concepts of *mistrust* and *distrust*. According to Citrin and Stoker (2018), *mistrust* "reflects doubt or skepticism about trustworthiness of the other," while *distrust* is a full, "settled belief" that the other cannot be trusted (p. 50). In this book, I use the terms interchangeably, but using Citrin and Stoker's definition, we can see that distrust explains why some people just don't and might never trust their boss.

So how can principals build trust with people who aren't predisposed to give it? The first thing to do is focus on where these people are coming from. What contributes to the mindset that principals are untrustworthy? Factors vary, depending on the stakeholder group you ask.

Teachers' perspective on a principal's trustworthiness is likely to be influenced by factors such as

- The character, tenure, strengths, successes, and challenges of the school's previous principal;
- The teacher's positive or negative perception of their long-ago childhood principals; and
- The overall culture of the district or school regarding administrators. Are they seen as an exclusive club of taskmaster bosses, as servant leaders, or as something in between?

Students' willingness to trust the principal are often influenced by

- What they hear their parents say about the principal, the school, and the teachers;
- What other students say about and how they behave toward administrators;
- Attitudes they see modeled by teachers and staff; and
- The individual student's interactions and experiences with teachers and the principal.

Finally, the degree to which parents and members of the community trust in the principal is influenced by

- The experiences they had when they were in school themselves;
- Community and social media schemas about the school and principal;
- Staff and principal turnover that casts doubt on hiring practices and staff commitment; and
- Their child's past history in school.

The most challenging part of these trust-influencing factors is how hidden they are, even to those they affect. For example, a teacher with a long-running pattern of contrarian behavior around supervisors may not be conscious of deeply held biases against "people at the top." Students may enter school in kindergarten having been warned against interacting with the principal. Parents may carry resentment from interactions with their own principal that occurred decades ago and in a different school system. Principals sometimes experience negative treatment that is aggressive or hurtful yet *completely invisible to those who are delivering it;* this is just how bias works.

Being Trust Willing

Being trustworthy is a positive character trait that is drummed into our minds from the time we are very, very young. *Be honest. Work hard. Do the right thing. Show character and integrity.* We know how it feels when others trust us, and years of ingrained social pressure and training have taught us how to work toward gaining others' trust.

What is just as important, though, and harder to identify if we have it, is a willingness to trust others. Unfortunately, many principals go into their job assuming they *can't* trust other people. There are myriad reasons. I remember the graduate program in which I got my principal certificate. The classes all tended to teach aspiring principals how *not* to trust others—it was like a three-year master class in all the things that could go wrong for principals if they let their guard down. *Unions will try to get you fired. Teachers will try to take shortcuts. Parents will undermine and attack you. Students will behave badly, disrespect you, and cause disruptions. News outlets will swarm like hornets if you do anything wrong. Legal challenges will be decided against you.* In other words, many principals have been implicitly trained to be distrustful.

It also can be difficult to trust others because the concept of hesitancy is constantly reinforced in us. Many times, district supervisors hold principals accountable when problems rise to the district office level. Parents hold principals accountable when their children have problems. In other words, even the most natural, predictable situations—such as common mistakes made by students and staff—reflect poorly on the principal. The belief seems to be "Why didn't the principal handle this problem?" This is quite unfair, as many times there is nothing the principal could have done to stop a problem, but it does perpetuate a low-grade fear within us that we shouldn't trust others because it might backfire in the form of negative judgment or reprimands. We hesitate because we're never sure who, or what, to trust.

And then there is the reality of actually taking a risk and trusting someone . . . and getting burned for it. I once walked into our school's resource room and heard a group of teachers talking negatively about me. At the center of the conversation was a teacher I had respected, admired, and trusted. I slunk out of the room, and to this day I'm certain they didn't see me. Hurt and stunned, I walked down the hall and through the lunchroom, where I stood for a moment to gather my thoughts. Seeing a table of students getting loud and rambunctious, I leaned down and asked them to stop. They did. As I turned to leave, though, I happened to look over at my shoulder and caught a glimpse of a couple of students imitating me, their faces twisted and mocking. I felt like I'd been punched. Overcome by hurt twice in the span of five minutes, I went into a custodial closet and wept, swearing to myself I wouldn't trust anyone ever again. Not at work, anyway.

Incidents like this are common, so it's no wonder many principals are hesitant about trusting others. I have since gotten over that terrible day, and if I ever relive something similar, I know I will handle both situations much differently. I will let the teachers know I hear them. I will ask how I can make a better connection with them. I will kindly but firmly ask the students not to mock or imitate me. And most of all, I will not take a really bad five minutes and use it as a reason to swear off the art of being trust willing.

Why be trust willing?

I know, now, that principals must trust others, even when relationships with the people they trust are not perfect (which relationships are?) and with the expectation that there may be hurtful moments. There are two main reasons why I encourage myself to remain trust willing.

To Lighten the Load

Principals have a very full plate of complex, ever-changing responsibilities. I've never met a principal who can effectively do it all without help. That's why turning certain tasks over to others is so important. Trusting others to take some of the leadership load is the only way to truly manage it all.

I know a high school principal who should be overworked and overwhelmed beyond measure; he has an incredibly complicated building with several thousand students. Pressure is intense, parents are deeply involved, and the community has extremely high expectations. Yet this principal always seems completely in control; he is calm, organized, and exudes confidence in his leadership. Why? Because he isn't doing all the work alone. He has an outstanding team, and he lets them take things off his plate. His assistants have clearly defined responsibilities, all of which are published for students and staff to see. Teachers have formal and informal leadership roles, and he trusts them to handle their jobs without input or interception. On his school's website, there is a visual depiction of all staff members with their areas of responsibility, and it shows parents whom to call for various problems. This principal is an able facilitator, but he does not insert himself into small, day-to-day decisions.

To Continue a Circle of Trust

When we empower others to own their work, to anticipate and accept the repercussions of their missteps, and to take responsibility for their professional reputation and legacy, we are effectively saying to them, "I believe in you. I will step aside and let you handle this, and when you succeed, I will celebrate alongside you." When we do this for others, they want to be deserving of that trust, so they work to validate it. In doing so, they also develop an appreciative trust in us, too. It's a circle. It feeds itself. So if we are trust willing, we will also be seen as trustworthy.

Let's think about the reverse, then. When a principal feels they need to micromanage the professionals on staff, or to speak to students and parents—in tone, action, or mindset—as if they do not deserve a voice in decision making, it raises a wall of instant defensiveness. *Why doesn't my principal believe in me? Why do I feel dismissed and disvalued? Why does my principal treat me like a child?* If a teacher, student, or parent is thinking these thoughts, they will not be likely to put their own trust in the principal. It stops the cycle before it even starts.

This is why principals should work to be open and willing to trust others. To measure how successful we are in doing so, let's do some self-reflection. It is never easy to honestly check in on yourself to determine how others perceive your leadership, but there are a series of questions we might ask ourselves in order to audit our ability, willingness, and ease of trusting others:

- *Do I have faith in the people with whom I work?*
- *Do I get anxious when other people are in charge?*
- *Do I believe serving students and parents is part of what I do, or am I thinking of them as adversaries or barriers?*
- *Do I micromanage and control others by checking in frequently or offering my opinion when it is not needed?*
- *Am I quick to criticize work that does not align with my approach?*
- *When there are challenges, do we encourage our people to do what is right and then get out of the way, trusting they will handle it?*
- *Do I understand and accept that others might approach a situation differently than I would?*
- *When others disagree with me, do I assume they are wrong?*
- *Do I believe others' mistakes will reflect poorly on me?*

Being willing to trust others feels like a leap of faith, but when we make that leap, it can be immensely freeing. We can think, with relief, *I don't have to do it all on my own. I am surrounded by people who are competent and capable. If I'm able to lean on others, I don't have to do it all myself.* Again, it is a cyclical self-feeder. If we trust others and they rise to the occasion, we trust them more. At the same time, because we have invested our trust, they reciprocate: *My principal believes in me. With that vote of confidence, I believe in my principal. Therefore, I trust my principal.*

Ways to show teachers and staff members you are trust willing

There's an easy, three-part formula for demonstrating trust willingness: *Let them lead, elevate their voices, and give them chances.*

Let Teachers and Staff Lead

As explained earlier, there are two reasons to empower teacher leadership: it lightens the heavy load administrators carry, and it creates a self-feeding cycle of trust. Principals can show their belief and faith in the professional skill of their teachers by actively seeking ways they can lead.

Many schools have formalized leadership roles—department heads, team leaders, advisors, principal advisory teams, PLC leadership, and so on—but there are countless other ways to give teachers and other staff members opportunities to lead. I used to run an "Idea Factory" each year at a summer staff retreat, and we'd all share dreams and goals for the year. When staff proposed new initiatives, my first question would be "Who can help lead an exploration of the feasibility, impact, and sustainability of this idea?" Not all ideas came to fruition, but when someone had an idea they believed in, they were instantly empowered to research implementation and determine the feasibility and sustainability of the idea. It created automatic embedded leadership. As an example, about 10 years ago at one such retreat, a teacher raised the idea of implementing a daily video announcement show. When the rest of the staff showed their agreement, two other teachers raised their hands to help, making a team of three teachers who had identified themselves as the point people for the project. It took almost eight months to get it off the ground, because those three teachers needed to spend time writing grants for the appropriate technology, developing criteria for students to be on the video team, planning the template for the announcements, determining how the news would stream into each classroom, and then, ultimately, rolling out a fantastic news program. It still exists today.

Elevate Teacher and Staff Voices

When teachers provide perspective, insight, and opinions, it's important to value what they are saying and give them the time and environment to share. Some principals have built in office hours, schedule reflection time at staff meetings, host individual conferences, or find other ways to make themselves readily available to hear what teachers have to say about the school, the students, and the way the system works. It's also important to let them use their voices, literally. I once attended a school music concert with a friend and noticed the principal did all the talking. All of it. *I would like to introduce these students.... I have always valued musical performances.... When I was a student, I was a proud member of the choir and orchestra....* He even stepped up with additional concluding remarks after the show, seeming to take credit for the successful performance: *When I approved the program for this evening, I knew these students would do me proud!* The music teachers were never given a chance to speak—and neither were students, by the way. The entire concert could have gone on without the principal commandeering the microphone—and it would have shown the music teachers he wanted them to own the show and get the credit for it, too.

Give Teachers and Staff Chances

When we talk about being trust willing, that doesn't mean we should have blind faith and certainty about every teacher all the time. Teachers and staff will break our trust, perhaps unknowingly and perhaps unintentionally. When this happens, it doesn't mean we write them off forever. If a teacher breaks trust, it's best to take note and move on, especially if it happens just once or twice. Of course, a pattern of behavior might cause a principal to perpetually distrust a staff member, and that's OK—as long as it isn't a general distrust of all staff members. And for those few staff members we aren't able or willing to trust, it doesn't mean we treat them with dismissal or disrespect, and it doesn't mean we still don't empower them to be in some leadership roles.

Ways to show parents you are trust willing

Principals can use the same three-part formula to demonstrate trust willingness toward parents.

Let Parents Lead

Some parents want nothing more than to be left out of school-based leadership. They want to send their children to school and leave it at that. They have no desire to be involved. I was one of these parents with my own children; I found my principal work left me with leadership fatigue in other settings. I didn't volunteer, I didn't lead parent committees, and I stayed pretty quiet. I supported my children and their teachers, I attended events, and I donated to the PTO, but that was the extent of it. Many parents fall into this category. Yet there are also many parents who want to be actively involved, and many have a strong leadership background and skills. For these parents, if there is a system for them to lead though parent engagement groups, it will give a structure and platform for principals to listen to their questions or concerns. The most common example is the PTO or PTA, but many schools also have specific volunteer opportunities, booster organizations, or parent groups to support a particular culture or demographic. To support these initiatives, principals should avoid doing too much for them. Instead, we should be part of the groups, with a seat at the table, but avoid stepping in and taking over as a "boss." We should offer insight and support—a process that will help them vet their ideas and determine if their ideas fit with the school's mission and focus—but we should avoid making decisions for them.

Elevate Parent Voices

Even parents who are not highly involved or engaged want to know they are valued and will be heard. Giving parents a voice can happen on a micro level, wherein parents know their phone calls will be returned and their emails will receive a response; it can also happen on a macro level, wherein parents are invited to give feedback and produce helpful ideas for the school as a whole. As stated above, engagement groups are quite effective, especially when the communication is two-way—the principal shares information and initiatives from the school, responds to questions, and then gives parents an opportunity to share their perspective. This isn't to say it's easy. I have sat in many a parent meeting where some of the ideas and proposals were not feasible, appropriate, or manageable (the proposal to have margarita trucks at an elementary school event comes to mind, as does the parent who had strong recommendations on how the school handled discipline, particularly in situations that included her child), but I have trained myself to listen, understand, and graciously deny some of the requests that come my way. Many times, new ideas can be incorporated into preexisting events and programs, allowing a natural evolution and improvement of long-standing traditions.

It's worth noting that there should be commonsense guardrails put on this. A parent who is abusive, toxic, or spreading misinformation should not be given a microphone to amplify their negativity. But most parents do not fall into this category, so we want to make sure they have a voice in an appropriate and helpful way.

Give Parents Chances

I was an inexperienced principal when I was hired to lead a large neighborhood school near where I had been a teacher and assistant principal. Not long after the school year started, a parent approached me in the car pickup line. Her son had gotten into her van with a cut above his eye. She was furious and quickly made it personal, going after my leadership and supervisory skills. I was stunned speechless by her rant but managed to listen and cobble together a response about looking into what had happened. I didn't know this parent; a teacher later told me her name.

Back inside the school, I asked the secretary if this was normal behavior from that parent, secretly vowing to write her off as a crazy, volatile parent who should not be trusted.

"Goodness, no," the secretary replied. "She is usually very calm and supportive. That reaction is very out of character for her."

Surprising. I silently told myself to withhold judgment until I had gotten to know the parent a little better.

The next morning at drop-off, the parent actually approached me to apologize. As any principal knows, apologies from parents are rare, so I listened with respect as she explained she'd just panicked when she saw her son's injury. "It sounds like it was just a playground accident," she said. "I should never have acted that way."

In the months and years that followed, I learned that she was, indeed, a very calm and supportive parent. I was glad I hadn't jumped to conclusions about her and thankful there was a chance for us to move past this first encounter. Giving second, third, and fourth chances applies to many situations with parents; after all, they are just humans trying to do their best. They run late. They get emotional. They forget to sign things. They don't load money into the school lunch account. They forget to write a note for a dentist appointment. They don't check backpacks. None of these "slips" should lead a principal to distrust them.

I was much more prone to do this before I became a parent myself and learned how often parents feel they are barely hanging on. Now that my children are in school, forgiveness and chances from my own children's teachers and principals—and an ongoing willingness to trust me in spite of all my flaws—mean the world to me. I hope I can offer the same grace to parents of the children who attend my own school. I try to withhold judgment and trust that they are doing their best.

Ways to show students you are trust willing

The three-part formula—let them lead, elevate their voices, and give them chances—even works with students.

Let Students Lead

I once met a football coach who rarely spoke. Well, he spoke a lot on the field, coaching his heart out and leaving most game nights with a hoarse, barely functional voice. But during events like team meals, awards nights, and senior dinners, he did not speak.

The reason was simple: he believed in his players as the team's leaders, and he let them show it. It was incredible to watch. Leading up to an event, he frontloaded players with information and prepared them for their roles. During the event, he just sat nearby, his hat pulled down, and smiled as his players gave the speeches or led the ceremonies. It was the students who got the attention of the crowd, who got to thank parents for their support, who articulated positives and negatives about the season, and then, always, who ended by leading everyone in a raucous team cheer. The coach believed his players were the ones who needed to be heard. His faith and trust in them showcased what they were capable of if given a voice and a microphone.

This mindset can be applied to any situation in which students typically sit back as adults do all the work and take credit for success. We should focus instead on proper preparation—mentoring, guiding, and facilitating as needed—and then step aside so that students can take the wheel.

Elevate Student Voices

I love it when I hear principals working through a problem with teachers or colleagues and then point out, "We should pause on this so we can listen to what the students have to say." Student leadership teams and student advisory groups can provide important insight into what is going well and what needs to change. Additionally, asking students to take the microphone to introduce guest speakers, lead pep rallies, and highlight important parts of assemblies or performances is a big vote for the confidence we have in them—and also gives them practice with their leadership skills. I know a high school principal who has senior leaders plan every single assembly and town hall; she meets with them to align goals, then she steps aside and only facilitates if students ask for help. I know another principal whose school has multiple cultural representation clubs, and he assigns them specific initiatives to oversee. He organizes opportunities; they take over from there. When we listen to students and respond to their concerns, we show we trust them as legitimate stakeholders in our school's mission.

Give Students Chances

I recently worked with a principal who was engaging in restorative practices with a student who continually got himself in trouble. "I'm impressed you haven't given up on this student," I said to the principal. She grinned. "Aww, he's not finished yet," she said. "He's just a kid. Got lots of time before he's all done cooking." This principal's understanding that students are still "works in progress" freed her to trust that the student would, with time and support, become someone who didn't need as much intervention. The principal had her eye on the long view and was open to giving the student multiple restarts and retries. Again, there are caveats to this—sometimes students run out of chances, such as when school policy outlines a particular number of infractions before a change in placement—but many times, students benefit from time and opportunity to grow.

How to Promote Trustworthiness and Trust Willingness

Now that we've considered how being trustworthy and trust willing might look, let's think about ways principals can be both. Below are three ways we can incorporate trust in and for others into our daily professional practice.

Modeling

Like many people, I sometimes fall into the trap of talking negatively about others. It's easy to do under the guise of venting. A student with a discipline issue, a parent who has been unreasonable, a teacher who repeatedly makes missteps or leaves colleagues in the lurch—these are all common reasons I have grown frustrated and need to let it out. Of course there needs to be a way to process our negative feelings with others, and it is healthy to plan a response with trusted colleagues. But it's easy to fall into a trap in which every challenge is met with an instinct to bad-mouth another person. A principal I once knew always referred to students as "knuckleheads" and "fools" and "delinquents." At first, he did it to be funny, but I think he came to believe it. In time, his administrative team and teachers mirrored similar language when they spoke about students. It was disturbing on many levels, not the least of which was the principal's inability to see that he'd unintentionally reinforced a culture of mistrust between all members of his school community. I overheard him tell a parent once, "You know what your juvenile delinquent did today?" He went on to explain a minor lunchroom incident, but the look on the parent's face showed she didn't know whether he was joking or serious, and her responses to him throughout their conversation were hesitant. The two of them never got to a place of authentic conversation, because the parent was on guard with the terms he used to describe her daughter.

Leveraging relationships

Not long ago, I was speaking about the importance of modeling to a small group of principals, and I told the story of the principal who used disparaging terms to describe his students. I was surprised when she pushed back.

"Sometimes we have relationships with parents, and we use language that might seem disparaging, but it is actually meant to be an endearment," she explained. She was an assistant principal of a high school and frequently spoke with parents she knew well using terms she knew would connect with them. When I asked for an example, she said, "Just this morning I called a parent and said her kid was acting like an idiot." I grimaced, but she continued, emphatically. "I would never say that unless I knew the mother and had a previous connection with her, but I knew it was the right language to use. The mother laughed, and we had a great conversation about his actions and consequences. I know this parent well. If I had been too formal—'I'm calling to tell you about a poor choice your son made today'—it would have had her on guard."

Coding our language to match the relationships and understanding we have built takes wisdom and skill. After all, both these things can be true—we should model professional language, but we also need to know how to connect with those with whom we are communicating. At the root of it all are the relationships of trust and connection we have with others. As mentioned in Chapter 1, part of gaining that trust involves being authentic in who you are and establishing rapport, connections, and symbiotic understanding with others.

Forgiveness

"Trust is like an eraser. It gets smaller with every mistake." While this observation (from an unknown source) may be true for big mistakes or repeated infractions that are genuinely harmful, in most cases, I find this mindset to be troubling. Mistakes are just that—*mistakes*. We all make them. Principals who lead schools with strong trust cultures understand this. They set expectations and do everything they can to make sure their systems are set up to benefit students. But when something happens, forgiveness comes first, then a plan to help overcome it, and then an effort to move on. By the same token, when principals make errors in judgment, an apology and a promise to try not to repeat the mistake—even if it's a private promise—will, if the apology is heartfelt and the promise is met, create a willingness of others to join the trust cycle.

In thinking about reciprocal trust, I find it helps to imagine trust as an actual structure. I picture a tall, strong, formidable building that can withstand storms, weather, and the weight of its responsibilities. I imagine sturdy pillars that hold the building in place. In this imagining, I also picture what happens when trust breaks: these pillars develop cracks and fissures that need to be patched up. At times, especially if there are few pillars rather than many, the building comes tumbling down.

This vision is a metaphor for principals and the way they think about trust. Just one pillar won't hold up an entire building; we need multiple trust pillars working together to be as strong as possible. In the next chapter, we will re-create this image and discuss how we can avoid trust killers and build trust pillars.

Before we dive into that, though, let's wrap up this chapter with another acknowledgemnt of the powerful role trust has in a principal's successful leadership. Becoming a principal who is both trustworthy and trust willing is a symbiotic process. When principals look to teachers, parents, and students with an eye for letting them lead, elevating their voices, and providing ongoing opportunities of forgiveness and growth, we model the relational importance of trust.

Trust Pillars and Trust Killers

We closed the last chapter with an image of trust pillars—what it looks like, what it feels like, and what happens when the "pillar" becomes a "killer." I started imagining "trust pillars" and "trust killers" while watching the construction of a large hospital near my home. It took a very, very long time—several years of deliberate work. First, the construction company sunk massive steel structures deep into the ground. Next, they built reinforcements, wrapping each structure. A crane lifted and placed crossbeams floor by floor; as the structure rose into the sky, mechanical elements, electrical ones, and plumbing went in. The finished building looks formidable, and I expect it will be standing strong long after I am gone. Still, while the hospital was being built, there were so many things that could have gone wrong. If the architects hadn't drawn enough pillars to hold the structure's weight . . . if the crane operator had been off in judgment and slipped when placing the original pillars . . . if the crossbeams hadn't been placed properly . . . if the excavation team had not done a thorough and permanent job laying the original pipes and cables . . . if an electrical connection had sparked and burned. All kinds of small missteps could have delayed, compromised, or even destroyed the structure.

This is how I imagine trust—as something that must be carefully built from the ground up. If trust is nurtured and watched over, it will become a strong, long-lasting structure. A "trust pillar" holds the weight of school leaders' relationships, mission, and future challenges. Most people *want* to trust their leader, and they welcome reasons to do so. And when their leader falters, as human beings invariably do, people can be remarkably forgiving if trust pillars are standing strong.

Yet trust is never immune to damage, and in that sense, it is always at risk. Breaking promises, treating people poorly, or failing to honor confidences are all examples of what can become a trust killer. To complicate matters, trust killing is generally unintentional, and many principals aren't aware of how their words and actions are damaging, even breaking, trust with colleagues, staff, students, and families. Some may even be unaware how much broken trust can undermine everything good they are trying to do.

As mentioned in Chapter 2, we will revisit our "why" throughout this book with reminders of a principal's ultimate goal of supporting students and enhancing their academic and social growth. Research tells us there is a direct correlation between principal behaviors and student achievement (Liebowitz & Porter, 2019; Tschannen-Moran & Gareis, 2015). Bozman's 2011 meta-analysis points out that both teachers' trust in the principal and the principal's trust in teachers (demonstrated by cultivation of teacher efficacy) improves student graduation rate, ACT results, and scores on English, reading, and mathematics assessments. The conclusion? Principals should be accountable for the establishment and maintenance of trust with the faculty, students, parents, and the community (Bozman, 2011).

According to researchers who reviewed literature on trust in a school environment, there are multiple "faces" of

There is a direct correlation between trust and multiple measures of student achievement.

trust. These faces, much like the pillars we discuss in this book, apply to relationships with the principal, with colleagues, and with "clients" (the community served by the school). The first is a general *willingness to be vulnerable*. The others are *benevolence, reliability, competence, honesty,* and *openness* (Bukko et al., 2021; Hoy & Tschannen-Moran,

1999). To this list, I'll add one more, based on my own experience: *professionalism*.

When we think about principals' efforts to be both trustworthy and trust willing, these pillars of trust provide an excellent framework to get us started. In this chapter, we will look at seven scenarios to examine how a principal might mishandle them, unnecessarily (and perhaps unintentionally) turning trust pillars into trust killers. Then, we'll flip the image to consider how the principal in each scenario might turn trust-killing behavior around.

Trust Pillar: Willingness to Be Vulnerable

Keisha was honestly surprised to find herself a principal at 28 years old. When she applied for a vacant position in her district at the urging of her superintendent, she didn't really expect to earn the job. Throughout her first year, she felt a bit like an imposter. Did she know enough? Was she experienced enough? Where could she find a network of support and camaraderie? These questions were difficult to answer, especially because it seemed every person she met in her new school made some sort of remark about how young she was. "I never had a principal who looked like you," one parent told her. "Aren't you, like, just out of college?" one of her students asked. "How did you land a job as a principal so early in your career?" a fellow principal wondered.

Feeling anxious and insecure, Keisha reached out to the mentor her district had assigned to her, a seasoned principal who had been one of the district's first female leaders. Keisha's mentor didn't mince words: "You're going to have to work twice as hard and be twice as tough to get half as far as the men in this organization." When Keisha's eyes widened at this, her mentor just shrugged. "And be careful not to appear weak," she added. "They're looking for you to fail."

Keisha left the meeting resolved to succeed, no matter what. She taught herself to stand ramrod straight and speak with complete conviction. Whenever a staff member questioned or suggested adjustments to any of her changes or initiatives, Keisha insisted on staying the course, even when there was obvious confusion or things weren't going well. "You cannot look unsure," she would remind herself. "You cannot waffle or seem weak." Keisha even resisted turning to her school counselors or teacher leaders to guide and support her. Behind Keisha's back, her staff started calling her "the Robot" and joking about her being a heartless and unyielding administrative machine. A student overheard teachers commenting on "the Robot," and word spread quickly. Soon students were using the nickname, too. Someone even made an Instagram account full of photos and memes mocking Keisha.

When Keisha finally stumbled across the account, she was crushed. She wept in her office, so upset that her secretary, a woman 20 years older than Keisha, stepped in. Seemingly a supportive and maternal friend, the secretary suggested she go home early. Keisha agreed, packing her bags and leaving for the day. The secretary, even though she had recommended that Keisha go home, was surprised that she'd just . . . left. It didn't seem like a very "principal-like" thing to do. When a teacher asked where Keisha had gone, the secretary whispered the whole story of Keisha's meltdown. "I can tell you this," the secretary said, wrapping up. "She is not going to make it." The teacher agreed. "Yeah. She acts so tough, but she can't cut it."

It's ironic, isn't it? By trying *not* to be vulnerable, Keisha made herself even more so. Indeed, if Keisha hadn't worked so hard to hide her insecurities, perhaps she would have been given a bit more humanity and grace by her school community. Of course, a principal *does* need to have presence and be firm and confident when making decisions. But these two qualities, toughness and vulnerability, can coexist. Here are a few ways to integrate them to build trust:

- *Admit uncertainty.* "That's a new one for me," Keisha could have said when presented with a difficult question. "I'm going to think about it and ask a few folks some questions; I'll get back to you."
- *Rely on a team.* Creating a team of teacher leaders on whom she could rely would have helped Keisha learn about her school, the staff, and the community of learners. The team could have shared some of the burden Keisha was carrying and served as support when things got difficult.

- *Don't run away.* When Keisha left early that day, she'd been encouraged by the secretary, and this felt like "permission." But the secretary was not in a leadership role or a position of authority; she also proved to be the kind of "friend" who would share Keisha's struggles with someone else. The lack of trust between Keisha and the secretary fed the perception that Keisha was running away from a problem. It also created an imbalance of power, giving the secretary control of the narrative about Keisha's abilities.
- *Pause to recalibrate.* Rather than giving in to the emotional overwhelm that day, Keisha might have excused herself to go on a walk, gather her thoughts, and prepare a response that would be based on strong leadership. She might have told herself, "I am full of feelings right now, and I need to step away from them. I'm going to identify a task I can tackle right now to distract my mind." This would have helped Keisha reclaim some sense of calm and purpose. Ironically, by accepting her vulnerability and working alongside it, Keisha could have elicited respect and trust from those around her.

When Keisha returned to school and realized her secretary had talked about her and characterized her leaving as a weakness, she took time to think about her potential responses. She realized she couldn't change that perception, because for her staff and school, leaving had, indeed, been running away from the problem. Rather than get angry, Keisha decided to admit to her complicated feelings. Imitating a phrase she'd heard from a friend, she started to acknowledge difficult moments by saying, "OK, everyone. I'm 'all up in my feelings' right now. I might need a minute." She poked fun at her nickname, too. "I respond to anxiety by acting like a robot. Bear with me while I try to open my human side."

Simply acknowledging the criticism against her seemed to deflate it. Keisha's staff appreciated her willingness to work on being more open and honest about her insecurities.

Takeaway: Refusal to show vulnerability is a trust killer. Trusted leaders are able to show their human side and admit to mistakes, and they don't try to be the know-all and end-all.

Trust Pillar: Benevolence

Donte, a veteran principal, was approached by Marina, the president of the district's bargaining unit (teacher's union). Marina told Donte several teachers in his building had reported feeling increasingly stressed, overwhelmed, and pressured. "I'd like to brainstorm potential solutions," Marina explained to Donte.

Donte barely let her finish before his own stress kicked in. "I'm tired of hearing how 'stressed' teachers are," he said. "They should toughen up. I was a teacher for years, and I guarantee you I never whined or complained like they do."

"Well, they're not whining or complaining so much as they are trying to manage a lot of new initiatives," Marina said.

"Oh, come on," Donte retorted. "They have a great job with a lot of time off. And they are paid well—in fact, they make more on their per-diem rate than I do. I would love to have the perks they have. Maybe next year I ought to move everyone to a new grade level and give them all new class preps? That would give them some legitimate stress rather than all this made-up stress."

Marina ended the meeting quickly, and when she went back to the school's union representatives, she told them she felt sorry for them for having to work with a principal like Donte. "He's negative, he's unkind, and he doesn't want what's best for you," she told them. "Watch out for yourselves, because he's not going to be a guy that watches out for you." Instead of killing trust as Donte did, he could have approached the problem brought to him with kindness and an intent to be helpful and find solutions. When he heard from Marina that teachers were feeling stressed, overwhelmed, and overly pressured, he could have responded in a more productive way:

- *Pause.* Asking Marina for a few moments, hours, or even days to prepare his response would likely have resulted in something more sensitive and helpful.
- *Ask more questions.* Rather than give a dismissive, definitive response, Donte might have sought understanding:
  - "Tell me more about the stress. What is the source?"
  - "Is the pressure coming from our own teaching staff or outside factors?"

- "Are you hearing from just a couple of teachers or the larger group? Are there subsets of teachers feeling it more acutely—particular departments, grade levels, or specialization areas?"
- "Are there any teachers you feel could join us in a meeting to discuss solutions?"
- "What can be done in the short term to alleviate this stress? How might we solve this with a long-term lens?"

- *Work collaboratively.* Bringing Marina in to help tackle the problem and generate solutions would create an environment of purpose and teamwork. Donte might have said something like, "I hear you, and I know you are a problem-solver. What can we do together to address this problem?" The resulting conversation could have led to a plan that got real results.

Donte broke trust with Marina in ways that are difficult to overcome. To remedy the situation, he would need to reflect on the damage done and be willing to change his mindset. A follow-up conversation with Marina, in which he admits that his own stress had made him incapable of empathizing with his teaching staff, would help reveal his intention to understand and accept the struggles and stress in his school.

Takeaway: Unkindness, negative judgments, and spite are trust killers. Trusted leaders are kind, compassionate, and well-intentioned.

Trust Pillar: Reliability

"I love this job," Sherie, a middle school principal, used to say at every opportunity. "I'm having so much fun that this doesn't even feel like 'work.'"

Sherie long assumed comments like this inspired her students, staff, and community, but she was wrong. Everyone found it annoying. To them, it sounded like overcompensation. They knew what Sherie couldn't admit: she gushed about loving her job to divert attention from the fact that her staff and community couldn't trust her to be steady, present, and reliable.

Sherie had always struggled with executive functioning skills, though it wasn't that much of a problem until she became a principal. She had been a productive and well-liked teacher, and she was especially successful during the years she had a very close teammate. "We fit each other perfectly," she remembered. "My strengths were his weaknesses and vice versa." But once she was in a leadership role without a teammate, Sherie struggled—especially with balancing her demanding job with raising two daughters through a shared custody agreement.

She arrived late almost every day, forgot important documents, and failed to communicate in a concise and productive way. She didn't keep up with emails or voice messages. Sherie's secretary reminded her about important calendar events, but Sherie often forgot to attend or showed up poorly prepared. She even looked disheveled, sometimes even wearing a different shoe on each foot. "I'm a mess!" she often joked, chattering to cover up her anxieties about her forgetfulness. Secretly, she hoped admitting her struggles—showing her vulnerability—would be endearing. Sherie's staff knew she tried very hard, but they also knew they could not depend on her, and that undercurrent of frustration increased over time.

Unfortunately, simply "trying harder" is unlikely to address the underlying issues we see in this principal's case. A better choice for Sherie would be to address the core of her problem, which is unreliability. Here's where she could start:

- *Make a list of priorities.* Working with a coach, mentor, or trusted colleague, Sherie might list the aspects of leadership in which she *must* be reliable and then make those her highest priorities. What matters most to the student experience? What do teachers really need from her?
- *Delegate.* If there are items at the top of the priority list that Sherie just can't manage, someone else may be able to pick up the slack and do the job well. In exchange, Sherie might find ways to balance the workload of the people helping her.
- *Look for other answers.* Sherie is at risk of being more and more isolated if her reliability doesn't improve, because her school community's frustration could shift into resentment or anger.

Realizing this, Sherie might commit to modifying her approach to the job, her priorities, and her responsibilities. She could identify tools and scaffolds to help her meet her responsibilities, just as she might have done for a student in her classroom.

In actuality, Sherie's unreliability continued to snowball. The worse she felt about it, the worse she performed. Eventually, her supervisor met with her, outlined his concerns, and set a specific timeline for improvement. Mortified at being on a formal growth plan, and facing the real possibility of losing her job, Sherie consulted a psychiatrist, who tested Sherie for ADHD and determined she had many indicators—impulsive, disorganized, easily overwhelmed, and prone to careless mistakes and getting lost in daydreams or unrelated projects. Sherie joined an ADHD support group and started medication, both of which helped her develop specific strategies to improve her ability to complete tasks.

Takeaway: Unreliability is a trust killer. Trusted leaders are responsible and dependable.

Trust Pillar: Competence

Over Malik's first decade as a principal, he worked in five different school districts, always with the same career goal in mind: become a superintendent. Yes, he worried some that his résumé gave the impression he was job hopping, but he figured that if he could just find the perfect principal gig, he'd be able to tap into the professional network he needed—people with connections who could vouch for the quality of his work. Every time Malik started a new position, he got excited about getting a step closer to a superintendent job.

But a negative pattern emerged. Malik's first year at a new school always went relatively well, but sometime during the second year, his staff would grow disgruntled. Tensions would rise. Teachers would complain about him and then involve the union. District leadership would step in, but Malik always felt that the central office's support was half-hearted and didn't really help. And then, just like clockwork, his supervisors would suggest he begin looking for a different job.

Confused and more than a little frustrated, Malik began working with a professional coach. "I want to be a superintendent," he explained, "but I haven't gotten any support or mentoring from any of the districts that have hired me." Prompted by the coach to reflect on why he had bounced around so much, Malik came up blank. "I just don't know," he admitted. "The staff seems to love me at first, but then they just . . . turn on me. I'm not doing anything different the first day than I'm doing the last day." When the coach asked Malik about feedback from his supervisors, he shrugged. "They imply I don't know what I'm doing—like I need to know more about running a high school. It's insulting. Of course I know how to be a principal!"

Together, the coach and Malik began a review of his evaluations, going back 10 years. The first one indicated Malik had struggled to make a workable master schedule, resulting in inefficient use of teaching staff. The next said Malik had not provided appropriate feedback on teacher evaluations, relying instead on a cut-and-paste method wherein most teachers received the exact same responses. Another said Malik should familiarize himself with district norms and protocols before making decisions. Notably, for each evaluation, Malik provided a rebuttal to explain why the evaluator's feedback was unwarranted.

The coach paused, then gently suggested that Malik wasn't hearing what his supervisors had been trying to tell him: that he has a problematic lack of knowledge about operations, instruction, and school protocols. Moreover, his reaction—to argue with the evaluator's assessment—signaled an intention to stay in a place of incompetence rather than commit to learning and growing.

Malik was insulted. "I'm not incompetent!" he insisted. "It's they who have a problem with me."

"Careful," the coach said. "I hear you responding with arrogance and stubbornness. You can turn this around, break this pattern, but you first have to admit to your weaknesses."

We see what Malik's coach saw: he needs to put his ego aside and examine why longevity seems to be a problem for him. Malik should use what he's learned from past evaluations and have honest conversations with his current supervisors. Avoiding being defensive is crucial here, so Malik will need to avoid blaming, being defensive, or avoiding culpability. Here are a few steps he might take:

- *Review.* Malik would benefit from going back and studying all previous evaluations with openness rather than defensiveness. What messages were his supervisors really trying to convey?
- *Reflect.* He might also think critically about previous conversations, emails, and communications with staff members over the years. What issues did they raise? What was the nature of staff frustration?
- *Examine.* When finding specific complaints, Malik should examine what they might mean about his leadership. This will involve responding honestly to questions like these:
  - *Do I know as much as I should about how to develop and implement a master schedule? If not, what are my options?*
  - *How do I approach difficult conversations with staff?*
  - *What do I do to build trust with my teachers and department heads?*
  - *Do I follow through on my promises?*
  - *Is the feedback I provide helpful?*
  - *Am I willing to dive in and learn about content unfamiliar to me?*
  - *When I am uncertain, do I ask questions and seek support or try to bluff it?*
  - *Do I pretend to understand situations, processes, and protocols when I really don't?*
  - *How do I ask for help?*
  - *How difficult is it for me to admit I don't know?*
  - *What support is available to me through my district? How might I access it? What can I do to get better and qualify myself for consideration for a superintendent position?*

Malik has a choice to make—to admit to the weaknesses others see or to insist they don't exist.

It actually took a warning from the district's central office to get Malik to really listen. "You do not have the skills to be a lead principal yet, much less a superintendent," he was told. "Until you master the competencies of your current role, we will not recommend you for any other position. In fact, you will be placed on an improvement plan so we can track your progress." Shaken, Malik went back to his coach and admitted he was afraid of losing his job. This fear translated to a willingness to slow down on pursing his ultimate career goal and first focus on mastering his current position.

Takeaway: Incompetence is a trust killer. Trusted leaders understand their job responsibilities and are well-equipped to meet them. They take responsibility for shoring up their weaknesses.

Trust Pillar: Honesty

Bret, a seasoned principal with plans to transition into district leadership, found himself speechless at the district human resources representative's news: several teachers on his staff had filed formal complaints about his dishonesty. They felt he lied to them routinely. They also cited situations in which Bret had not been honest with a parent about a child's behavior or discipline consequences. According to the report read aloud by the HR rep, "The principal seems to want to avoid conflict, so he chooses to soften or gloss over difficult information with things that just aren't true."

Bret was crushed. He had never meant to be dishonest. In fact, whenever he shared information that wasn't exactly accurate, his intention was to protect staff members from information that might be hurtful, maddening, or not applicable to their work. He said as much to Erin, the district HR director. "Sometimes people want to hear things that are none of their business," he told her. "That's why I tell them something innocuous. It's a way to push their questions away."

"But withholding accurate information—assuming it isn't confidential information, of course—can be perceived as a lie," Erin replied.

Bret thought a moment, then said, "I feel like my staff and community framed me. They asked me things I didn't know, and so I'd give guesses or predictions that they must have interpreted as facts. Later, when those things turned out to be the opposite of what I'd predicted, they thought I was lying. I wasn't!"

"But why did you say anything at all?" Erin asked. "If you didn't know the answer, why didn't you just say so?"

"Because a principal should know all the answers to any question," Bret replied.

Bret's reputation of dishonesty originated in a misconstruction of the principalship. He felt so certain that he needed to be an expert in all areas that he took liberties with the truth in an attempt to appear he was a confident, informed, all-knowing leader. Bret never had ill intentions, but after many incidents of sharing information that proved to be untrue, he had damaged his relationship with his staff.

As the complaints against him were investigated as incidents of dishonesty, Bret suspected he might not recover from the damage. He made the difficult decision to leave education. It was a drastic choice and one he does not regret, though he is still sad about the way his school community, in his words, "turned against him," and wishes it all would have been handled differently.

What Bret could have done, and what he should have done long before a full career change became the best option, was reflect on why his staff and community felt he wasn't honest. Here are some of the lessons he might have learned:

- *If you don't know, just say you don't know.* Many principals feel they truly should know everything about everything, but that's simply not feasible. Rather than try to "save face" with partial or believable bits of the truth, it's best to simply say, "I don't know the answer to that question. I'm so sorry." The conversation can end there. Or, if you do know some information, you might reply, "I don't know enough about the situation to speak to it." Choose silence over dishonesty. Other ideas are "I can't talk further about that" or "Unfortunately that's not something I'll be able to talk about."
- *Don't hoard information.* If Bret had noticed that a lack of certainty was making staff members anxious, he might have assuaged their worry by keeping them in the loop. He could have prefaced his comments with a caveat—"I don't know much, but I'm happy to share the small bit of information I have" or "There's only a few things that are confirmed, but I will communicate with you as soon as more information becomes available." This kind of transparency from a leader helps to reassure

the community that they will have the information they need when they really need it.
- *...But be sure to honor confidentiality.* If you're ever asked to keep something confidential, that's what you should do. Requests for information you don't have, or for information you're not at liberty to share, are better met with frankness than avoidance: "I'm not the person who has [or can share] that information, but if anything changes, I will let you know."
- *Choose delayed truth over instant answers.* Again, it's OK to tell people, "I don't have that information," or "There isn't enough information to share quite yet," or "This process is going to take some time to work out," or "I want to be certain about this information, so I ask you to check back with me in a few months so I can be accurate with what I say." In other words, even though it might feel better to give an answer every time you are asked a question, it's best to always choose the truth, and the truth is sometimes something you have to wait for.
- *End conversations if there's nowhere for them to go.* If someone is pushing for information that shouldn't be discussed, the best strategy is to let the period at the end of the sentence be the end of it. Think of the "No further comment" approach taken by many public figures. If said with a friendly tone, it will end the conversation without further incident.

For teachers, students, and parents, interactions with Bret left them feeling insulted—as if they couldn't be trusted to hear the truth or he didn't respect them enough to share information with them. They had learned to see Bret as dishonest, and dishonest people can't be trusted.

That's what happens when principals, with all good intentions, don't tell the truth. It may be something as simple as fudging the facts or downplaying details about a student's discipline infraction, or as large as giving an inaccurate explanation about an instructional resource rollout. I've seen principals change information to fit a positive narrative rather than be open and honest about the information and then revisit the positive narrative. In most cases, the truth eventually emerges . . . and serves as an instant trust killer for a principal who didn't use it.

Of course, rarely is a principal deliberately dishonest. Indeed, I have never met a principal who says, "Ooh! I can't wait to tell a couple of lies today!" But in a job largely built around the successful distribution of information, it can be confusing to know when to communicate, how to communicate, and how much to communicate. It is simpler to tell the truth the first time. That doesn't mean you always say everything you know. In some cases, the best way to preserve truth is to avoid saying anything at all.

Takeaway: Secretiveness and deception are trust killers. Trusted leaders are honest, clear, and straightforward with accurate information.

Trust Pillar: An Open Mindset

Tracy knew that education is a field that is always evolving, but he had an instinctive resistance to change. As a principal, he was known for saying no and for pushing back against suggested innovations, Tracy didn't think of himself as close-minded, pessimistic, or especially conservative; he simply wanted to protect his teachers from taking on burdensome initiatives, changes, and responsibilities—and protect his students from distractions that could compromise their learning. So, whenever parents approached him with an idea for a community night, he said no because he didn't want teachers giving up yet another evening for work responsibilities—they already did so much! Whenever a teacher suggested trying a new resource or purchasing a flashy new tool, he suggested first mastering the current set of resources and tools. Whenever students came to him with ideas (develop a new club, create a volunteer group, host an event), he dragged his heels and tried to find ways to postpone actions and decisions.

Tracy did all this for what he told himself were good reasons. His staff and students were struggling to manage all that they already had on their plates. But his refusal to entertain new ideas was (rightfully) perceived as a closed mindset. "Don't even ask," members of the school community advised one another. "He'll just say no."

By closing his mind to change, Tracy may have been protecting teachers from burdensome initiatives, but he was also turning away from tactics that might have made his school and the people in it, adults *and* kids, better and more efficient teachers and learners, more excited about the work ahead of them.

A mindset of openness makes space for new ideas, new initiatives, and, most important, a community that is accepting and excited about the future and meeting the challenges it may bring. Tracy might try the following tactics:

- *Start with yes.* Instead of defaulting to no and setting others the task of talking him into changing his mind, he could flip that: start with yes and then think about and talk about possible limitations, setbacks, and strategies for making the plan work.
- *Consider the impossible.* Rather than put his guard up, Tracy could open his mind to wild thinking and "what ifs?" that build excitement, encourage risk taking, and might lead to the school doing things he'd never thought to be possible.
- *Welcome conversation.* Rather than shut people down, Tracy could ask questions (and follow-ups to) to uncover ways that would support his priorities rather than distract from or undermine them. This means replacing "That will never work here" with "OK, interesting! Tell me more... and tell me why!"

Tracy's instinctive "no" needed pushback, and a group of teachers decided to provide it. A few of them, identified as leaders by their peers, came to him to have a formal conversation. "We feel like you kill any new ideas we have," they said. "We need a way to communicate our ideas that won't immediately be shut down." Although it took Tracy time to accept their message, he eventually admitted he needed to be more trusting of his school community. He relied on the teacher leaders to hold him accountable in opening himself to listen, think, accept ideas, and dream alongside them.

Takeaway: Rigidity or close-mindedness is a trust killer. Trusted leaders welcome fresh, innovative thinking and are eager to lead growth and positive change.

Trust Pillar: Professionalism

After 10 years in the classroom, Devin applied for the role as principal in her building. As someone with long-standing relationships with the school community, experience as a teacher leader in the school, and years of friendship and camaraderie with her colleagues, she was the favored candidate and got the job. But soon after being named to the position, the outgoing principal gave her this warning: "Listen, this is a lonely job. Make sure you cultivate a network of administrator colleagues from other schools so you always have someone who knows and understands how you're feeling."

Devin wasn't worried. She was certain she wouldn't feel lonely—not with so many friends on staff. Throughout her first year, she worked hard to prove to her staff that she could be both a supervisor and a friend. She set up a professional development schedule and asked her former teammates, whose instructional leadership she admired, to serve as models of practice and provide tips to colleagues. She followed up with teachers she felt were not as instructionally sound, inviting them to observe the master teachers at work. She sensed a little resistance but continued along, making sure all teachers had the resources and materials they needed. She monitored the morale and moods of her staff by asking her previous teammates, who were still her close friends, how things were going. Devin attended happy hours, staff parties, and showers thrown for weddings and babies, and she stayed all the way to the end. She even carpooled to work with one of the teachers on staff (another of her former teammates), spending the daily drives talking about challenges the school faced, team dynamics, and even the good gossip. When that teammate came down with strep throat, Devin stepped in to sub in her classroom, working extra hours at night to catch up on her own tasks. Isn't that what friends are for?

As Devin moved into her second year, though, many of her friends on staff were feeling awkward about her connection to them. She sensed a coldness from staff members in other grade levels, the ones she hadn't worked as closely with when she was a teacher. Everyone was polite, but they kept a distance. When Devin brought this up to her friends on staff, they quickly changed the subject. Her carpool friend was the most direct: "Listen, I can't talk to you about this, OK?" she said, then suggested they might begin driving in separately. It felt like a breakup, and Devin was shocked by how heartbroken she felt. Not long afterward, she walked into the staff lounge and noticed how her arrival stopped a lively conversation cold. Then, right before the holiday break, she received an email that had not been intended for her. The staff was planning a party, and she was not invited.

Devin remembered the warning about the loneliness and realized, with a shock, that she was deeply lonely at work. *They don't trust me,* she realized. *The lack of trust is so deep that they are deliberately leaving me out. They don't want to connect with me. Have I ruined everything?*

Professionalism is the triple threat of trust pillars for principals: it equates to being fair, equitable, and connected to your staff. It's hard to imagine a principal setting out to be unprofessional, but most professional educators have at least encountered behavior from leaders that we would describe as such and that act as trust killers.

Devin never intended to be unprofessional. In fact, in her eyes, she was *being* professional by maintaining her friendships with her professional friends. What she didn't realize was how her actions had created a culture of inequity and preferential treatment. Her commitment to staying close with her former teammates did not account for the difficult position she was putting those teachers in, and they eventually grew uncomfortable enough to establish the distance between them that Devin had not.

The good news for Devin is that she can reverse the trajectory and begin building a trust pillar. She might start by acknowledging her missteps and articulating her plan going forward. Here are a couple mindset shifts she might consider:

- *Focus on equitable treatment.* Devin had close friendships with certain staff members at the expense of others. Her friendships exacerbated inequities, and they increased opportunities for particular staff members over others, all of which compromised Devin's professionalism and weakened trust. Trust is built when every teacher feels they have a place, a value, and a voice in what they do. Each teacher must know they will get what they

need to be successful and that they have the appropriate opportunities to excel.
- *Connect with principal colleagues.* Principals *do* have a lonely job. Or, better said, their jobs might easily be lonely if they rely on a previous, outdated set of relationships and don't work toward professional growth. To overcome this, a principal like Devin might consider actively building a network of other principals or administrators. Having a few people with whom she can process information, share ideas, and connect experiences will take the place of "teacher friends." That isn't to say principals shouldn't be friends with teachers; rather, they should handle these friendships with grace and even a little distance from the professional requirements of leadership.

Devin was able to reflect on her professional journey and how her previous friendships factored into her future goals. In time, she realized she needed to grieve the change in relationships that had accompanied her shift into the principal role—but she also realized this situation wasn't an isolated one. Indeed, many of her friendships had evolved over her lifetime. Friends from high school, college, and graduate school had changed with the years. With this perspective, she was able to let go of thinking her "teacher friends" were her only option. Devin begin actively making different connections with others who were in a similar professional situation.

Takeaway: Unprofessionalism—even when unintentional—is a trust killer. Trusted leaders are professional, fair, and equitable; they don't play favorites.

Trust and the Responsibility Leaders Bear

As mentioned earlier, trust pillars can't work in isolation; they interweave, support, and feed off one another. Furthermore, the seven discussed here are not all-encompassing. There are certainly more, especially in a school setting that is so fully immersed in human interactions. A few others that come to mind for principals are *clarity, visibility,* and *availability.* Take a moment now to think about the trust killers for these trust pillars and some of the ways they might manifest in your work.

As we wrap up this chapter and think more about all these scenarios, you might be feeling a heavy responsibility. *Is trust that much of a weight to carry?* you could be wondering. *Is it that easily broken, and does it really take that much time and effort to build (or rebuild)?*

I believe most people are generally forgiving, and most want a trusting relationship with their principal. I have made thousands of mistakes in my work as a principal, but I've also found it to be a rare scenario in which I couldn't recover. When I admitted to my mistakes, articulated a plan, and approached my work with a fair, professionally giving heart, trust would settle into place beautifully. I don't think of establishing and upholding trust as a "task" for a principal to complete; it is a mindset and a commitment, a feeling and a practice. Trust is an outcome, too—a gift in some ways but also a result (and a lovely one!) of all the other decisions we make. In that sense, strong leaders do not think of trust as a heavy burden but as a foundational state of being.

Strong, trusting relationships are crucial to school success, because a culture of trust leads to more effective collaboration and decision making, along with a sense of safety and membership in a moral community. (Kutsyuruba et al., 2010). This is the type of school environment that will support teacher efficacy and student growth.

> Building a school's culture of trust will support overall collaboration, learning, and community.

My friend Margo is a firefighter. When I first met her, she told me how she'd decided to attend fire training school and build a life around being a first responder. Her story fascinated me. "When I graduated from college, I knew three important things about myself. First, I loved working as part of a team. Second, I wanted to make a difference. And third, and probably most important, I needed to trust the people with whom I worked." When considering what career to pursue, Margo repeated her "Big Three" over and over to whomever would listen.

One day, a friend heard what Margo was looking for—a job with teamwork that is focused on making a difference and conducted within an environment of trust—and suggested she do a ride-along with a firefighting team. She did. The very next day, she enrolled in firefighter training. Twenty years later, Margo is still fighting fires and loving all aspects of her career. "I love that when we go on a call, we all have a specific role. We go into the situation knowing our job extremely well, and we know how to look out for one another as they do their jobs. We don't get in anyone else's way unless asked." She thought for a moment. "It all comes down to trust."

Margo's description of a firefighting team parallels the way a school team should work. We all have our specific responsibilities, and we should be trusted and empowered to do them well. At the same time, we should feel surrounded by support from our team and know we can count on them to help us if we get into trouble. Feelings of competition, threats, loneliness, and fear should not be part of our daily work. And, as Margo said, it all comes down to trust.

4

Trust with Teachers

I used to think principals should just hire the right people, put them in the right positions, and everything would work out. "Hire well, and get out of the way," as the saying goes. And while that is partly true, teachers can be limited by the conditions of the system they are hired into. If policies, practices, frameworks, efficiency measures, or operational management is weak or dysfunctional, even the most talented and committed teachers will struggle to succeed in the face of barriers, red tape, and outdated or inapplicable systems.

In his book *Schools Cannot Do It Alone*, Jamie Vollmer (2010) makes a similar observation. Teachers are highly educated and bring to the profession a deep desire to do right by students, but they face multiple systematic barriers, including "audiences comprised of diverse, distracted, demanding children, many of whom are victims of a pop culture that overstimulates their physiologies, fractures their attention spans, and promotes a bizarre sense of entitlement" (p. 5). While Vollmer's words certainly mirror the tendency of one generation to look upon the upcoming generation and despair—*They're so spoiled!*

They don't know how good they have it!—it's worth noting because generational differences add to other issues teachers face: the layers of bureaucracy, lack of funding, and a critical public. All contribute to a systematic challenge that has the potential to lead teachers and principals toward burnout. Strategies and systems that educators learned 10, 20, or 30 years ago may no longer be a good fit with today's reality.

Conversely, developing new systems to accommodate the various components of a mid-21st century classroom—behavior management, academic differentiation, tiered support, and a demanding community of stakeholders—can have a profound, positive effect. Principals are in the unique position of needing to be in the vanguard of instructional thinking while also needing to honor the expertise of their teachers and develop manageable systems to support both. They must bring their schools to a level of operation that will support teacher growth, increase student achievement, and provide positive measurable outcomes.

It's a lot to manage, but it becomes infinitely easier with reciprocal trust in, and for, teachers. Research tells us that principals who foster and maintain trust enjoy improved faculty collegiality, instructional leadership, school climate, teacher professionalism, community engagement, and student achievement (Tschannen-Moran & Gareis, 2015).

> The level of trust that a staff has in a principal is related to staff collegiality, instruction, and student achievement.

"System Health" as an Aspect of Trust

In addition to the trust killers we have looked at so far, staff also lose trust in their principal when the principal's leadership doesn't develop, feed, and support a strong system. It may be a lack of a thoughtful professional development plan. It may be a fragmented or inconsistent response to student behavior. It could be an unclear or unfair budget allocation. When a problem arises, if the system that is *supposed* to solve it has weaknesses, teachers will respond with frustration and dissatisfaction.

Not long ago, I worked with a group of Canadian principals. During a small-group conversation about school culture, a disagreement arose. At issue was one principal's lament that all the work he was doing on instructional leadership, all his efforts to support positive growth and change, were being met with resistance. This principal (I'll call him Ryan) shared that his teachers talked about him behind his back, spreading negative energy throughout the school and making him the scapegoat for any problems that arose. "It's like they want things to stay as they always have been, want to keep using resources and strategies that were cutting-edge 40 years ago. When I push them toward something more modern, they get really angry at me."

"You need to develop thicker skin," another principal in the group told him. "It's totally normal for staff to resist change and to talk about you behind your back."

"No, it's *not* normal," a third principal interjected. "It might be *common*, but it's not *normal*."

What followed was a lively conversation about the normalizing of negative school culture, including distrust among staff and for leadership that creates division. It becomes a mindset of *us versus them*, with the administrators on one side and the teachers on the other. Whenever there are two "sides," there is competition to "win" or to be "right." Feelings of ill will, resentment, and anger in a school setting can damage an entire school community, overtaking any positive intentions that anyone might have.

With this in mind, I listened to the principals as they discussed the normalization of unacceptable behavior. After a few minutes, I asked a question: "What if the reason teachers talk about their principal is because they are frustrated by a broken system?"

Silence.

"Ryan, you say your people are resistant to change," I continued, "but perhaps they are actually resistant to the style, approach, or timing of the changes you're implementing? Let's think about the professional development plan you've set for them. Maybe the teachers are insecure about their knowledge of new teaching strategies. Or maybe your building doesn't have good Wi-Fi, which makes it a hassle to integrate the technology in the ways you've requested."

The principals looked thoughtful. "So, let's think about this," I continued. "What if Ryan got to the root of the systemic resistance? For example, what if he created a team of teachers to brainstorm a different approach to professional development—one that fits their needs?"

Another lively discussion ensued. Ideas flowed. "Send a few teachers to a cutting-edge tech conference and have them lead some PD," someone said. "Ask a couple teachers to develop a PD schedule," someone else offered. Others chimed in: "Create a system of collaborative classroom visits so teachers can watch one another." "Set up visits with another school." "Write grants." "Rethink the training teachers have been given to implement their resources." "Team up with a nearby principal to share PD expertise."

I loved the ideas, and I was excited to see the principals shift away from the symptoms of the problem (gossip, resistance) and toward the problem itself (subpar staff training). I did offer a caution, though. "Listen, teachers *are* going to talk about the principal," I said. "But if they have a clear vision of the principal's plan, and if there is buy-in from most of the staff, it won't feel so divisive. They'll still judge you, but it won't be in such negative terms. And it won't become a habit." I told the group that it reminded me how a friend of mine, who had reluctantly shared her home with her mother-in-law for a few months, felt unexpectedly unmoored when her mother-in-law finally moved into her own condominium. "Who am I going to complain about *now*?" my friend had asked, half-laughing at herself and half-serious.

Processing information with others is natural. Doing it with a perpetual negative lens, though, isn't helpful, especially when it's covering a larger systematic problem. Regardless, trash-talking is a modeled behavior—if it is done often and freely, and its normalization becomes universally accepted, trust will be broken to the point where it will be very difficult to repair.

So trust needs to be firmly in place. Systems create trust. Honest and open dialogue about challenges within that system also creates trust. After all, we all share the same mission. Teachers and principals are in this together; we are allies, not enemies.

A Closer Look at Fractured Trust with Teachers

As principals, we work alongside our teachers, both literally and figuratively. We set goals and policies, but we also serve our staff by doing what we can to make sure they have what they need and leading them toward professional mastery. When we find out they have done something to sabotage, damage, or compromise our professionalism, it can cut especially deep.

Let's dive into a scenario of compromised trust between a principal and teachers. We'll consider what the principal might do in this situation, before going on to discuss various ways a principal might increase reciprocal trust within a school.

Misaligned Goals

Clairie is a principal in a large urban district with a strong union presence. When she took the job, her colleagues warned her that she would not have "real" leadership power. That was held by Roxanne, a longtime teacher and the union's building representative. Roxanne, they said, would be the one with the influence, clout, and decision-making power. But Clairie didn't pay the warnings any mind; she had experienced working with unions and had always gotten along well with teachers and union representatives. She knew she wanted to lead improvement of instructional practices in the school, and she couldn't imagine how the teachers could object to the goal of more effective instruction.

In her first few months at the school, Clairie worked hard to establish strong relationships with her teachers. She was thoughtful and intentional about connecting with Roxanne. They spoke often, and both appreciated the culture of trust they were building together.

As the year progressed, Clairie began to notice there were several teachers who did not have a full courseload. They had multiple study hall periods, or "student support" time, but the principal didn't see them doing any actual . . . teaching. Two of them—longtime staff members—actually left the building for several hours each day. Clairie suspected no one had taken on this problem because it was "the way it's always been." But their reduced responsibilities had created deep inequities among staff members in terms of workload, deadlines, and stress. So, in the spring of her first year, during a monthly check-in meeting with Roxanne, Clairie pointed out the disparities and suggested they could probably cut two or even three full-time positions, saving the district important operating dollars.

"If we reallocate these particular staff members, will we be able to keep the positions in our school and use them for something else?" Roxanne asked.

Clairie was confused. "No, we would lose those positions," she said. "The teachers would be transferred to another building." Seeing the expression on the union rep's face, the principal added, "But losing the positions shouldn't be a problem. Clearly, we don't need them. We don't have the enrollment to support them. And clearing them from the books will save the district hundreds of thousands of dollars."

"I couldn't care less about the district and saving them money," Roxanne snapped, gathering her things and standing up to leave.

"But . . . we are 'the district,'" Clairie said. "And it's my responsibility to—" But Roxanne had left, closing the door behind her. Clairie wasn't sure what had happened, but she was glad she'd had the conversation and was eager to share this plan for greater fiscal responsibility with her supervisor.

By the afternoon, though, Clairie could sense a chill in the air. Making her rounds, she noticed teachers were avoiding her. During afternoon bus duty, two teachers walked the other way rather than speak with her. "Word's out," her secretary told her.

"Word's out?"

"Everyone is buzzing that you're going to eliminate jobs."

Eliminate jobs? That's not at all what is happening here, Clairie thought, incredulous. Her idea was to simply reassign a couple of teachers to a school that needed them.

The situation did not blow over. The next few days brought emails from angry staff members accusing her of trying to "fire people" and "hide this under the guise of saving money." The tone of the emails was aggressive and angry.

Upset that Roxanne had misconstrued her intent and her words so badly, Clairie planned morning visits with several department heads to clear up the issue. But when she arrived in her office the next morning, before she could even put down her coat, her phone was ringing. It was her supervisor, and he was furious. "Why am I getting phone calls about you?" he sputtered. "What's going on over there? You're shaking up the staff? Firing teachers?"

Clairie tried to explain, but he cut her off. "Listen—stop. Just stop. We're not cutting any positions," he said. "Where did this come from? Are you just creating issues to get people all worked up? Your job is to keep things off my plate, not add to them."

She was stunned. She'd been trying to provide the best service for students across the district, spreading job responsibilities in a way that would be a better use of staff time. She'd communicated with Roxanne in an attempt to collaborate with the union, thinking that a more equitable workload would garner its support. She never dreamed of this collective backlash or this misinterpretation of her aims. She never dreamed her supervisor would get involved or that he'd be angry with her. If anything, she thought her efforts would be appreciated.

Clairie felt demoralized and devalued. Most of all, she felt betrayed by Roxanne, whom she'd grown to trust and value as a professional colleague. The response had made her remember that warning she'd been given: that she would be the principal in name only and that the union's building representative would lead in more powerful and efficient ways than she could.

Clairie learned a great deal from the experience I've described. For one thing, she recognized that sincere efforts to build trust don't always succeed. She recognized that communicating doesn't ensure understanding, and that sometimes principals and their staff members are working toward different outcomes.

Even with hurt feelings and damaged trust, there are many approaches Clairie might take to address the situation in her school. Let's think about one that is unlikely to go well, one that would be acceptable, and one that is likely to have a positive outcome.

- *Bad response*: Confront Roxanne. Reprimand her for spreading misinformation. Vow to never again trust Roxanne or any union member. Go over the supervisor's head and talk directly to the fiscal department to get their buy-in on the savings. Continue with the initiative but attribute any negative outcomes to district leaders. In other words, lash out, dig in, and blame.
- *Good response:* Try to overcome resentment and call another meeting with Roxanne. Work toward a mutual understanding by again sharing the goal (improved efficiency, better instruction), having Roxanne repeat it back, and ask if Roxanne has any ideas for solving the problem of teachers with idle time. Then, meet with the supervisor to explain the intention, and proceed with the response the district recommends.
- *Most effective response:* Explain again, both individually to Roxanne and to other staff members who might be affected, what the long-term goal is—to improve efficiency and improve instructional practices. Slow down. Recognize that the misunderstanding—Clairie planning to eliminate jobs—originated in anxiety and fear; work to assuage these feelings. Make sure there is district support to re-allocate staff. Get input from staff members, which might include information about their licensure, their professional goals, and where they might want their career to go.

In this scenario, both Clairie and Roxanne (and the rest of the staff) felt betrayed. This feeling is not all that unusual in high-emotion situations. Principals might make a decision they feel is sensible and positive, then feel betrayed by an unexpected negative response from staff members. Similarly, staff can feel betrayed by a principal who makes a decision they interpret as being harmful. It's difficult for both to share the same broad lens. In any case, this demonstrates why principals should invest in trust pillars with teachers. It will have a correlative effect on teacher well-being, their instructional approach, and the school's overall organizational health (Liebowitz & Porter, 2019).

> A trusting relationship between principals and teachers will have a positive effect on instructional practices in the classroom.

Knowing that the principal-teacher relationship has a direct impact on a school's instructional strength, let's look at what principals can do to manage behaviors that have the potential to damage trust.

Trust Killers with Teachers

We'll start by revealing ways principals might be unintentionally compromising ("killing") trust with teachers.

Unclear or uninformed instructional expectations

As leaders, principals have an opportunity to combine the talents and skills of teachers into an overarching culture of instructional excellence. However, without a firm grasp on best instructional practices, it is difficult for a principal to be an effective instructional leader. Sometimes they try anyway, but this rarely works out well for anyone—staff, students, or the principal. Any disconnect between the principal's expectations (realistic or not) and teacher output can test trust. I've seen situations in which teachers are comfortable with what they teach, how they teach it, and how they measure student mastery. Then the principal announces that these teachers need to "evolve" or change their practice but is unable to articulate why or how.

This is why *clarity* is an important trust pillar. Teachers trust principals who understand effective practice and expectations for teachers, articulate them both well, and provide ongoing training yet remain open to varying teacher perspectives and are willing to collaborate to optimize outcomes. Without instructional trust, teachers will burrow down in their classrooms, closing doors to avoid being "caught" doing something they have been told (but do not believe) is "wrong." They will look for contradictions in the principal's leadership and respond to suggestions or feedback with skepticism or rebellion.

Too many new initiatives

As you may recall from the chart in Chapter 1 (see pp. 18–20), education is infamous for piling on responsibilities. It seems there are always new mandates to address, new approaches to master, and new tools and supplemental resources to try as we search for better ways to respond to challenges and meet student needs. I once worked with a principal who had introduced three different reading programs within three years. To teachers, however, constant additions to their workload and repeated pivots from one trendy solution to another signal a poor understanding of what they do and compromise their faith in our leadership.

Favoritism

As illustrated in the scenario in Chapter 3 (see pp. 61–63), trust is compromised when principals show favoritism for certain teachers. While principals will always have teachers they particularly admire, respect, and lean upon, alliances with certain staff members shouldn't lead to inequitable treatment.

You also want to avoid a culture in which teachers are held to different standards depending on the relationship they have with the principal. I once coached a principal through a dispute involving a teacher who had received corrective feedback and a warning that the next step would be a formal improvement plan. Although the principal was convinced the teacher in question was lacking content knowledge and a firm grasp of academic standards, there was no data to support this conclusion; on the contrary, the teacher had better long-term trend data than her colleagues. Privately, the principal admitted to me that the teacher he'd reprimanded was one of his "least favorites."

I pointed out if staff were aware that he'd separated teachers as those he favored and those he didn't, it would be a safe bet that anyone in the "not favored" column would distrust his leadership.

Lack of courage

Staff members need to trust that their principal will do hard things when they are warranted. Whether it is working through professional development decisions, establishing boundaries for an intrusive parent, or appropriately disciplining a student, staff will lose trust if a principal cannot step up and have these difficult conversations. This doesn't mean the approach needs to be aggressive, mean, unfair, or atomic—on the contrary, handling difficult conversations gently will develop the principal's reputation as someone who can say hard things with compassion and professionalism. The important thing is that the conversations happen. If not, staff will criticize the principal for ignoring or deflecting problems and will not respect the principal's avoidance or fear of upsetting someone. As a mentor once said to me, "If you lead as if you are scared of upsetting someone, you'll upset everyone."

Self-promotion

Sometimes teachers work hard on an initiative, plan, or event but then have to watch as their principal gets credit for its success. Although some stand up and seize the credit they deserve, even they may feel diminished and insulted. The trust pillar related to this situation is *professionalism*. A principal accepting unearned credit not only threatens trust between staff and leadership, but also decreases the likelihood that staff members will continue to work hard for initiatives. I once watched a high school principal discuss, at length, the impact he'd had on a summer learning institute. The problem? The entire event had been conceived, planned, and implemented by a small and hardworking group of teachers. The principal's involvement had been minimal. But when the event feedback was overwhelmingly positive, the principal began taking credit for both the idea and the outcome, bragging to his superiors, and posting on social media about "his" summer institute. Teachers were furious and resentful, seeing the principal as both dishonest and self-promoting—a definite trust killer.

Deception

Once when I was mediating a conflict between a principal and a staff member, I learned that the principal would frequently lean on what he called "plausible deniability." He believed he could get away with all kinds of trust-killing behavior—favoritism, self-promotion, incompetence—so long as he could cloud the issue enough to convince people he *might not* be doing these things. This damages the *honesty* pillar of trust. As I worked through the investigation, I concluded this principal might be the most mistrusted principal I'd ever encountered. While his behavior was extreme, relying on plausible deniability as a leadership tactic—essentially deflecting blame to others in the organization—is certain to destroy any hope of trust between teachers and their principals.

Breaking confidences

When someone tells a principal something in confidence and that principal turns around and shares the information, it is likely the whole story will get back to the person who asked for the privacy. Talking about others, especially sharing their secrets, is a trust killer for which there probably is very little chance of recovery, because it perpetuates a cycle of gossip and pits staff members against one another. Worst of all, it diverts staff energy toward interpersonal drama and away from where it should be—on student learning.

Lack of commitment

It's not uncommon for teachers to work at the same school for decades, which gives them a long-term investment in the school's success. Frequent principal turnover can definitely undermine trust in both school and district leadership, leading teachers to wonder every time how long *this one* will last. Mistrust gets worse if there's any hint that the new principal sees the school as a temporary stop on a climb to somewhere better, or if they are dismissive or indifferent to the challenges teachers are facing. "My principal has one foot out the door," a teacher once told me in explanation for why she didn't trust her principal. "Why would she care about us? To her, we're just a pit stop." The *reliability* pilar of trust comes to mind here, as does *availability*; if a teacher can't trust that a principal is fully committed, it's hard to trust in that principal's leadership.

Refusing feedback

Principals get feedback all the time, formally and informally. It can be exhausting to receive endless opinions and perspectives, but principals generally learn how to manage the volume of feedback by looking for consistent themes and responding to constructive criticism when they determine it will have a positive impact. The relevant trust pillar here is an open mindset—a willingness to listen to and learn from others.

On the other hand, not asking for input, or ignoring input when it comes, shows a principal's unwillingness to accept feedback. Worse, some principals actively deflect feedback, telling themselves that the perspective is coming from a flawed point of view. "They have no idea what I deal with on a daily basis," they might say, or "They only know a fraction of the 'why' behind my decisions." While this might be true, perception is reality, so if teachers *feel* something, it is real to them. Denying, ignoring, or dismissing their perspective will tear trust apart.

Relying on quick fixes

How many times have you jumped on a solution because it was the first thing that came to mind or the easiest or fastest to implement? Wanting a quick fix is completely understandable, but repeatedly relying on quick fixes can compromise trust in the same way that rolling out too many initiatives can. It suggests both a lack of competence (the inability to analyze a situation and determine the most effective solution) and a lack of professionalism (showing too little consideration for how a lesser solution might affect staff, students, and parents).

I saw this play out when working with a principal who was anxious about leading her teachers through changes in her school's numeracy instruction. Because she wasn't confident in her own mathematics content knowledge, she looked elsewhere for guidance, which led to the failed implementation of three different online math programs within two years; all had been "sold" to her by vendors who knew how to capitalize on her anxiety and lack of knowledge. Students, parents, and teachers were left confused, and there was little direction and cohesion. No one knew the long-term vision for mathematics instruction in the school, and there were no specific goals or benchmarks to measure outcomes. In this principal's haste to fix the problem by "outsourcing" a solution, she inadvertently created many other problems. Had she paused to anticipate all outcomes and then develop a long-term vision, she could have selected and committed to one program and then given teachers time to master and fully implement it.

Trust Pillars with Teachers

Now that we've studied certain behaviors that can kill trust with teachers, let's think about some ways principals can deliberately and thoughtfully build trust pillars. We'll start with strategies and approaches that will help teachers know you are trustworthy, and then we will go on to discuss ways principals can increase their own mindset of being trust willing as they lead their staff.

A principal's trusting relationship with teachers has a ripple effect on how teachers view their students. Teachers who trust their principals are more likely to have a positive perception of student engagement, which increases student achievement (Price, 2015; Tschannen-Moran & Gareis, 2015). Additionally, there is a correlation between overall school effectiveness and the level of the trust teachers have in their principals (Chughtai & Buckley, 2009).

> Research affirms that a trusting relationship between teachers and principals can improve students' overall achievement.

Here are some powerful and surprising ways to build trust with teachers.

Slowing down

For school leaders, most problems feel urgent, but few are as time sensitive as they first seem. To be clear, yes, there are some situations in which immediate action is absolutely necessary, particularly when it involves safety. Perhaps it is these situations, fortunately rare, that contribute to the constant sense of urgency many principals feel. We need to push back against this urgency instinct and instead seek a mindset of restraint, patience, and deliberation. Doing so increases credibility because it allows us to practice the *availability* and *visibility* pillars of trust—taking time to think, listen, hear, and ponder the actions that will lead to the most desirable outcome. This advice applies to new initiatives, but it also applies to small daily interactions.

I have a principal friend who was hired to lead a school that had a dedicated classroom to support students with intense behavior needs. He spent a couple days shadowing the outgoing principal and was dismayed to hear the school's walkie-talkie system screeching throughout the day, announcing crisis after crisis. He watched the outgoing principal repeatedly drop everything and sprint to wherever the problem was. One of the first things my friend did as principal was add a headset to the walkie-talkie system so that the details of every incident weren't broadcast to the rest of the school. He also set a "no running" policy for himself. Whenever he was summoned to respond to an incident, he made it a point to walk there, calm as could be. "Unless they tell me a life is in danger, I am going to walk at a deliberate pace," he told me. "I am going to exude confidence and intention." His demeanor effectively eased the emotional intensity within the building. "Nothing is going to be different, or better, if I get there four seconds faster," he explained. "But things *will* be better if everyone knows the principal is on the way and can be trusted to be a calm, careful, and thoughtful presence in the room."

Checking the rules before committing to action

Have you ever come up with a great idea or an on-the-fly solution to a pressing problem only to find out your great idea was *technically* a policy violation? This happened to a principal friend of mine. In an effort to support a grieving staff member after a beloved substitute had passed away from cancer, she agreed to name a building addition after the deceased woman. Then she learned her district's policy prohibited naming facilities except in very rare and specifically outlined circumstances involving years of "significant impact" at the "state or national level." When my friend realized her mistake, she explained the situation openly and honestly to her staff. They ended up honoring the beloved substitute by planting a tree on school grounds. But she was frustrated with herself for having taken action without doing her research into what was and was not permitted. "I didn't even consider that there might be a policy for this," she said.

Honest mistakes happen, but patterns of hasty action followed by necessary backtracking and revision can undermine staff trust in a principal's competence. Ignoring or not owning up to non-compliant policy can damage the staff's trust in a principal's honesty.

My friend was determined not to repeat this mistake. She told me, "I have to start assuming there is *always* a rule and looking for it before I make any decisions." This is solid advice. Know where to find the rules, read the rules, and discuss with colleagues how you'll be interpreting them. Staff should know that a principal is dedicated to following district norms—policies and guidelines—with fidelity and will only dissent or deviate when the policies are not good for kids. I will talk more about this later in the chapter.

Acknowledging mistakes

Just like teachers and students make mistakes, so do their principals. I used to think every mistake was a gigantic problem. I felt terrible every time I made one. I was certain my mistakes would define my career and even worried one might end it. I now know that the best way to handle mistakes is to acknowledge them, apologize if the mistake caused problems for others, and move on. Doing so fortifies the *vulnerability* trust pillar.

There are two parts to acknowledging a mistake. The first is internally accepting your culpability, and the second is publicly recognizing it and discussing what you will do to make things right. Sometimes, especially if the mistake was minor, there is no need to "make things right." I have amassed thousands of examples of little things I've done that only require an "Oops! I shouldn't have done it that way. I sure won't make that mistake again!" But I've also made bigger mistakes—the kind that require an apology, reflection, and a conversation about what I did wrong and how to move forward.

Many principals struggle deciding when to offer a formal public apology and when to just apologize to a couple individuals. Here are a few questions I ask myself in this situation:

- *How big is the mistake?*
- *Were people inconvenienced? Hurt? How many? Who were they?*
- *What kind of damage was done? Is it merely a frustration or annoyance, or did the mistake change working conditions, affect student instruction, cause problems between colleagues, or leave someone feeling unsafe?*
- *Did the mistake damage trust?*
- *How might the mistake feel to others? Have they moved on already, or is this something with longer-lasting repercussions?*

If answers to most of these questions are no or "not much," acknowledge and apologize for the mistake and move on; a quick conversation in the hallway is usually sufficient. Other times, it might take more. I've written before about a guideline I call the "10-10-10-10 Rule." I ask myself, "Will this matter in 10 minutes, 10 hours, 10 months, or 10 years?" If the answer is no to the first two 10s, I let it go. If the answer to the first two 10s is yes, I talk to anyone directly involved. "I'm so sorry for my role in this," I say. "I won't do that again." That takes care of it, and we all move on. But if the last two 10s get a yes—if it will matter in 10 months or 10 years, that's a mistake with significant, even grave repercussions. In those cases, creating a plan to repair the damage and communicating with everyone who is affected is the best course of action.

I'll share an example that includes both a mistake that risks damaging trust and a proper correction that repairs it. I once consulted with an assistant principal who also served as the school's athletic director. One night, he supervised a basketball game in which students in attendance were behaving poorly, being rude to the officials and members of the opposing team. He went home that night, embarrassed and furious, and shot off an email mandating that all teachers speak to their homeroom class about unacceptable student behaviors at sporting events. "*You* own this problem, too," he stressed. The assistant principal attached an emphatically worded document—a list of expected behaviors and severe consequences for forbidden ones—that students were to read and sign. Teachers were upset. They hadn't attended the event. They didn't know which students were at fault, what specifically those students had done, or the extent of their behavior. The teachers certainly didn't feel comfortable chastising all their students for the behavior of a few. After talking it through with his principal, the assistant principal sent a second email to his staff: an apology. "This is not something you're expected to address in class today," he wrote. "I sent the first email after a frustrating evening, and I apologize for filling your inbox with a problem that is not your responsibility. I am still considering how we can improve student behavior at sporting events. I welcome your ideas and suggestions. Again, I'm sorry for the impulsive email." Several teachers came down to say they appreciated the retraction and the apology. They reassured him that they'd understood his intent and offered to brainstorm solutions from a school-culture lens. One even attended the next sporting event to oversee student behavior and offer support.

Committing to improvement

When a trusted and credible principal makes a mistake, they will likely receive grace from others, especially if it's not the same mistake being made over and over again. My superintendent often says, "Everyone makes mistakes. Let's just try not to make the same mistake twice." Using every day to get better, smarter, and less prone to repeat missteps will build trust.

Having an auditor

How can we commit to not repeating mistakes? I believe in accountability partners—trusted colleagues who can point out when you're off track and help you avoid a misstep. It might be an assistant, a secretary, a partner, or a colleague. I have often asked my secretary to "catch" me if I'm in a mindset that will lead to mistakes. "Tell me when you see me moving too fast," I say. "Tell me when I am being impulsive or overly emotional." I also have several trusted colleagues with whom I can check in and review a draft plan of action to ensure I don't make obvious mistakes.

We can also set checkpoints for ourselves. When making decisions or communicating information, we can outline steps to follow—and actually write them down—as guardrails to help us stay on track. We can also keep internal checkpoints in mind to reinforce the trust pillar of *openness*: *Am I making decisions with a clear mind? Do I need to get input from others?* One of my favorites is the self-quiz many educators use with students: *Is it necessary? Is it true? Is it kind? Is it helpful?*

Seeing the various sides

Being trustworthy requires us to be impartial and fair, which includes listening to various perspectives and valuing each one. There is political nuance to seeing both sides of a problem or situation. I don't mean politics in the traditional sense but more as the core definition of "politics"—the activities and behaviors associated with people making decisions, paired with the distribution of power, resources, or status.

Principals do well when they remember that because people are often unintentionally thinking about their own status with the principal, the school, or the community, they carefully watch how decisions are made and determine if the principal is making them fairly. The *benevolence* trust pillar allows the principal to appreciate various angles and be able to articulate what they are. "I understand the situation this way," a principal might say. "This person thinks, feels, or believes [insert explanation]. The other person thinks, feels, or believes [insert explanation]. Do I have that correct?"

Asking for help

Most principals can remember when they themselves were teachers, and they can remember how important it is to have a principal who is reliable. When problems arise, teachers need to know there will be action and follow-through. They also need to know principals will do what they say and say what they do. Of course, it helps if we are honest about our limitations. A principal cannot be the absolute master of all, and part of reliability is getting the right support in place.

For example, I once worked with a principal who was asked by his district leaders to lead his school in a professional development session focused on an important curricular initiative. The principal knew the content of the training was far removed from his expertise area. He reached out to the district's curriculum department and asked for help delivering the training. To his staff, he said, "Someone from our district office will be joining us during this training to help me learn, so I'll be right alongside you as we figure this out!" I wrote earlier about the trust-killing practice of too much outsourcing of expertise, but it is perfectly OK to admit when something isn't in your skill set, especially if faking understanding—or getting it wrong—will let others down. In this situation, a principal asking for help reinforces staff trust by illustrating honesty, resourcefulness, and a commitment to staff, who deserve effective instruction as much as students do.

Seeking consistent and clear alignment of norms

The systems that guide a school, whether they are unspoken agreements or formalized policies approved by a governing board, might come in the form of rules, guidelines, procedures, plans, or protocols. Staff look to school leadership to interpret and implement these systems in a way that makes sense as "the right way"; they want to know what they're doing is the best way to serve students and support their success. A principal with a deep knowledge of rules, policies, and protocols and capable of explaining how they align with the school's values and support its goals and mission is reinforcing the trust pillar of *competence.*

I always encourage principals to adhere to the intent of the policies and procedures. I caution them to be aware of biases that could tempt them to make exceptions in some situations and not in others. This is not a call to be inflexible but a call to be consistent. If you differentiate your responses for some people in some situations, you must do so for all people in those situations—no playing favorites. If there is a zero-tolerance policy, it should truly be zero tolerance.

Fortunately, most policies are written to give principals discretion; language specifying that the principal is the ultimate decision maker is common. Adhering to the intent of the original policy will help ensure a fair and consistent approach.

As decisions are implemented, it is worth remembering that teachers appreciate knowing the "why" behind a decision. Although it's true that explanations can lead to difficult conversations or debate or even compound resentment from some, in most cases, clearly articulating what has guided your decision making—be it alignment to past practice, to protocols, to policy—is helpful.

Being open to listening

In my experience, teachers want a principal who is approachable: both visible and available. They do not want a principal who is too busy, distracted, or overwhelmed to hear from teachers and get invested in their struggles and successes.

There's one incident that stands out in my memory. After my first year in the classroom, I made the difficult decision to resign. I saw my principal standing outside at bus duty and asked if he had a few moments to talk. I was sick inside—nervous about taking up his time but also anxious about the decision itself. I was resigning because I needed to relocate for reasons that had nothing to do with the job. I was happy in my work, didn't want to leave the school, didn't want to move away from the lovely rural area where I was living, and didn't want to abandon the principal after just one year. Perhaps he read these complicated emotions in my expression. He immediately turned, and we went together into his office. He listened intently to every word I said before responding with a kindness and degree of understanding that brought tears to my eyes. I felt that he knew how difficult the decision had been for me, and that he did me the favor of making the conversation as easy for me as he possibly could.

When a teacher approaches and says, "Got a minute?" there will be times when you actually might not have a minute—or an hour, as the case may be. That's fine, too; you'll just need to set up a different time to talk, one when you can be sure there'll be no distractions. The trust-building move here is simply to reassure teachers you want to listen and that you care about what they have to say.

Honoring the teaching profession

In addition to being available to listen, principals should make a conscious, concerted effort to remember what it was like to be a teacher. Those who can't remember should ask! "Tell me more" is a great starter, as is "Can you explain what that looks like, feels like, sounds like?"

Sticking up for teachers and for the challenges they face is a sure path to a strong, long-lasting trust pillar. An excellent example, one many of us are attuned to, is the advice to take care of teachers by respecting their time—by canceling unnecessary meetings, say, or by making sure necessary meetings start and end on schedule. The "gift of time" when least expected is, indeed, a wonderful thing.

Here are some other small ways to reassure teachers that you know, understand, and honor their work:

- Step in to cover teachers' duties as needed.
- Preserve teachers' precious preparation periods.
- During standardized assessment windows, be the person who offers restroom breaks to the testing proctors.
- When substitutes are short, step in to cover a class.
- When you notice something needs to be cleaned, clean it.
- If there is confusion on a curricular standard, make time to sit down and deconstruct it.
- Make sure staff have the supplies they need and store these in a centralized, easily accessible location.
- Look for and eliminate any barriers that get in the way of teachers being able to deliver on their work.

My personal career trajectory solidified my appreciation for these kinds of actions. Four years after going into administration, I took a break and returned to the classroom. My son had just been born. and I was worried about my ability to be both a good mother *and* a good principal. It didn't take long for me to realize just how much I'd forgotten about the pressure and stress of being a teacher! When I returned to an administrative role the next year, I was newly committed to believing teachers when they expressed their needs. I promised myself I would never discard the concerns and feelings they brought to me. I also vowed to educate myself more about the changes in the curriculum, various instructional strategies, and ways to support differentiation. I pledged to set reasonable deadlines and show my gratitude for teachers' hard work. I have learned that when teachers feel their principals still understand what it's like to be a teacher, they are more likely to trust the principal to act in their best interests.

Keeping staff secrets

When a staff trusts a principal, they tend to be more open about sharing personal and professional information, goals, worries, and challenges. Holding someone else's story is a privilege, but privilege comes with responsibility. When teachers confide in me or otherwise tell me something important, I will always ask, "How do you want me to handle this information?" Sometimes I learn it's something that should stay between the two us. Sometimes I learn they'd like me to share it with others so that they don't have to. Here are some examples:

- *A teacher who had received a diagnosis of breast cancer.* When I asked her how she wanted me to handle the information, she said, "I have to start treatment immediately, so people will begin to wonder. I just don't think I'm strong enough to talk about it. Will you serve as the spokesperson and my main point of contact?" Over the course of her treatment, we stayed in close touch, and I kept the staff updated on her progress. I also spoke with students, sharing information that was developmentally appropriate for their age, and I proactively emailed parents to prepare them for potential questions their children might have. Every word I shared had been rehearsed with and approved by the teacher ahead of time.
- *A teacher who was blindsided when his spouse asked him for a divorce.* He told me because he was struggling with significant shock and was worried that he wouldn't be able to be present at work the way he wanted to be. When I asked him how he wanted

me to handle the information, he asked me to keep it quiet, so I did. When anyone asked me about him (changes in his professional appearance and behavior were noticeable for a period of months), I had an answer ready—one I had cleared with him. "He is going through a challenging time, and he will let you know details when he is ready, " I would say, calmly and kindly. "Any other information isn't mine to share." Every time, the response from the inquirer was understanding and respectful.

- *A teacher who had learned she was pregnant with triplets.* After several painful miscarriages and a long in-vitro process, she had passed the 15-week mark, and her doctors felt she was safe to share the news. When I asked her about my responsibility in her secret, she asked for a few minutes at our next staff meeting. She wanted to share her celebration with the staff but also wanted to give an in-person expression of gratitude for the way her colleagues had supported her in the past. Again, I was honored to be trusted with her secret and honored to find a place for her to celebrate good news on her own timeline and in her own way.

Practicing emotional regulation

One sure-fire way for a principal to be seen as trustworthy is to demonstrate that you have a handle on your emotional responses. It reassures teachers that we can remain calm, supportive, and professional no matter what is thrown our way.

I have learned it's possible to present as calm and professional even when your insides are swirling with emotion. I do this by acknowledging what I'm feeling—anger, frustration, fear, disappointment—naming it, and forcing myself to set it aside while I work through the problem. I promise myself, *You can deal with this disappointment later; focus on a solution now.* In most cases, the emotion has dissipated by the time I return to it, meaning I can see its lessons more clearly. Another tool is to repeat to myself, *My training has prepared me to handle this situation. I must be the calm one. People are counting on me.* I have even gone so far as to imagine myself as a robot, incapable of being distracted by emotions, for the time it takes to solve the problem. If none of those strategies work and I find I simply can't manage how my feelings are coming out in behaviors or expressions, I excuse myself and postpone my response until I can effectively self-regulate again.

Expecting resistance, showing persistence

Some teachers distrust anyone in authority. Perhaps negative experiences in the past taught them that supervisors are not to be trusted. Often there is very little that can be done to change their minds beyond patient, ongoing efforts to create trust pillars. In situations where I suspect I am not trusted, I try to prove the distrustful folks wrong. If I can, great; if I can't, I just keep trying.

Showing Teachers You Are Trust Willing

One of the most important things a principal can do to demonstrate their trust in staff is to share some of the responsibilities of leadership. We discussed this at length in Chapter 2 with the advice to *let them lead, elevate their voices, and give them chances.* Trusting staff to step in, step up, and be leaders has the added benefit of reducing the stress of responsibility overload. I love to work with principals to brainstorm ways they can share the load they carry. For many, this is a difficult task; they step into the principalship with the assumption they have to do everything, know everything, and oversee every last detail. But I promise them there is immense freedom, and even relief, in trusting others to take the reins sometimes. Let's think about how to ensure you're sharing the workload with others.

Avoid micromanaging

Principals who insist on being part of every decision, even the small ones, may unintentionally send the message that they do not trust their teachers to do things correctly. When teachers feel this, they will disengage—after all, it's no fun to have your ideas dismissed, challenged, or overturned.

Mentor and support

Mentoring and coaching teachers is fun, fruitful, and invests in a school built on collective efficacy. When asking staff to assume a new responsibility or leadership position, make sure to cover the processes they might want to follow. I recommend a "guide and release approach" wherein you offer range of solution strategies, help build and leverage the necessary skills, debrief after contributions, and celebrate staff for their expanding leadership work.

Delegate

No principal can do it all. Pairing a necessary task or event with a staff member who has the time, capacity, or appropriate ability demonstrates your willingness to trust someone else on your team to do the job well. I've seen fantastic examples of delegation over the years, such as appointing social media managers, developing a curricular scope-and-sequence committee, empowering teachers to choose instructional materials, and so on.

Yield to greater expertise

Part of being willing to trust teachers is honoring how well they know their content. They are the experts, and trusting them means not questioning their knowledge. If, for example, I plan to observe a teacher in a subject area I don't know well, my pre-observation conference with them always starts with "Tell me what I will learn about your subject area." Then I ask follow-up questions to help myself become a student of the day's lesson. I don't question their expertise or make them feel like I might know better—because I *don't* know better, and they *know* I don't know better. In another example, unless there is something egregiously ineffective about a classroom's layout, I avoid telling teachers how to set up their learning spaces. Unless the setup impedes learning, why intervene? Just as a chef doesn't want a restaurant's manager to set up the kitchen, a teacher doesn't want a principal to tell them how to set up their classroom.

Reinforce work collaboratively

Several of these suggestions might put extra work on teachers, which is why it is important that decisions be made collaboratively, through conversation and mutual agreement. We never want teachers to resist our efforts or, worse, to begin feeling resentful. As mentioned earlier, when inviting others to share in leadership decisions and oversee initiatives, teachers must have the ability to decline or pass on work that is outside their hired responsibilities. Many principals find success by explicitly cultivating a strong relationship with union leaders and having regular conversations to ensure work is distributed fairly and the principal is adhering to professional guidelines. It's also helpful to repeatedly reinforce respect and gratitude for those who share leadership roles.

Reinforcing your commitment to sharing leadership will, in time, become part of your school's culture. I once had a boss whose term for sharing leadership was "providing opportunities" for teachers. It became a good-hearted joke: "Watch out! She's coming down the hall with an opportunity!" But we teachers were honored when our principal asked for our help, and we appreciated her willingness to let us lead. Teachers who did not want to lead in a particular situation would simply decline the opportunity, and the principal would offer it to someone else, no hard feelings. But everyone knew she would circle back around the next time another "opportunity" emerged.

This chapter has offered multiple reminders of the value of shared leadership. Letting others lead—*trusting* them to lead—is a way for a principal to show their faith and confidence in and their collaboration with staff and teachers. Teachers deserve our admiration, respect, and empowerment. Schools benefit when principals share the emotional, physical, and professional responsibilities that come with being a leader. It is freeing, too, because it opens up both time and energy, making a more balanced and capable leader.

As we wrap up this chapter, though, let's clarify one important point. With school leadership, there really is such a thing as too many cooks in the kitchen. Multiple people attempting to lead is a recipe for confusion and uncertainty. Principals do the necessary work of coordinating the contributions of the administrative and teacher leadership teams into actionable school operations. Our model here is the wonderful folktale *Stone Soup* and the reminder it provides that there are plenty of ways that teachers and staff member can contribute to the school's overall mission beyond the ones that first come to mind. If we all share a small amount of our knowledge, time, energy, and excitement, it will create an experience that everyone can enjoy. This is the true value of sharing responsibility—and of trust.

5

Trust with Parents

As school leaders, we must also establish trust with the parents, guardians, and other custodial adults responsible for our students outside school. For the sake of brevity, I'll call everyone in this category "parents."

To many parents, school seems like an impenetrable structure—a castle surrounded by a moat that's deep and wide. Once the school day starts, the drawbridge goes up, and parents are standing on the far shore. Now, we don't want parents constantly showing up at school and disrupting the rhythm of learning, but it makes sense that we should try to bridge the moat through ongoing communication, good news and photographs shared on a private social media page, ample opportunities to enter the castle for special events, and so on—anything that helps parents feel welcome rather than alienated and apart.

On a popular Facebook group for educators that I follow, posts relaying negative interactions with parents are a daily occurrence. Possibly you, too, have picked up an increasing disconnect between school and home or noticed more parents questioning the intentions, decisions, and outcomes of their children's teachers. While external scrutiny helps keep educators customer-service minded, the accompanying "on edge" feeling threatens to wear us out.

Why is this happening? What is behind parental distrust of schools and teachers? There are many potential reasons, but I think three are particularly noteworthy. First, I'll remind you of the history covered in Chapter 1: parental distrust of schools is common in turbulent times, when their instinct to protect their child is on high alert. Second, it is an undeniable fact that a small percentage of educators behave inappropriately, lack dedication, or bring negativity to a child's learning experience; the distrust this creates in the larger system is very difficult to mend. Finally, we know the proliferation of social media has given parents a platform that is unique in history. Anyone is able to broadcast even the smallest frustration to a large and faceless audience who will reinforce it with a "like" or a heart, boosting the signal further.

There are many issues that could lead a parent toward distrust. Later in this chapter, we'll dive into a scenario that illustrates how painful it can be when a parent mistreats us, even when we understand that this mistreatment is rooted in that parent's fear and worry for their child. Mistrust can also be rooted in other places; issues of power, personal experience, gender, race, and ethnicity all affect a parent's reaction to a principal, both passively and actively. Regardless of the origin of the distrust, it points to the value of principals working to establish trust with parents.

Research confirms it's worth the investment. Positive, trusting relationships between families and schools improve results with student learning, achievement, behavior, and attendance (Francis et al., 2016a). They also increase reciprocal information sharing that improves the overall optimization of a child's learning experience, while reducing the barriers parents perceive in helping their child overcome learning challenges (Lake et al., 2018).

Reciprocal relationships of trust between schools and parents improve the student experience and increase the likelihood of student success.

The Characteristics of Positive School-Home Partnerships

Trusting relationships with parents are not independent of other trust pillars; on the contrary, they are best embedded inside the overall culture of the school. Moreover, the responsibility for the work doesn't fall solely on the principal's shoulders; it's much deeper than that because the entire staff has an integral role to play in working with parents. Teachers are the most visible school personnel, the ones with whom parents interact most often and authentically. When establishing their level of trust with their child's school, parents consider how inclusive the school is, if there is positive and inclusive leadership, and what opportunities are available for families to become and stay involved. They also look for evidence of positive outcomes for all students, regardless of ability (Francis et al., 2016b).

In a review of parent perspectives on school-home partnerships, Francis and colleagues (2016a) highlight four themes: *communication*, *belonging*, *competence*, and *family leadership*. Here are some simple questions to help you explore each of these themes in relation to your school:

- *Communication.* Do your families have regular communication from the principal and their child's teachers? Do they know who to contact if they are confused or uncertain about procedures or processes?
- *Belonging.* Does every child "fit" somewhere in the school? Do families feel heard and seen and valued? Are they considered and included when decisions are made?
- *Competence.* Are staff members well trained? Are they confident in their roles? For those who are not (yet), what systems are in place to support them and ensure students are well served?
- *Family leadership.* Are there opportunities for families to immerse themselves in the school's mission or activities? Is there a focus on building connections across minoritized parent populations based on race, ethnicity, and socioeconomic status? Is there a sense of welcome, empathy, and reciprocal respect for all families?

A principal might bring questions like these to leadership groups—teacher leaders, department heads, parent engagement groups, support teams—for discussion Typically, the answers are very illuminating. Any concerning issues that arise during these discussions can be a starting point for the creation and development of a response plan.

A Closer Look at Fractured Trust with Parents

In spite of a principal's best efforts to have trusting relationships with the parents of students we serve, it's wise to accept that some will be predisposed to pushback. Most school leaders know what it's like for a conversation with parents to turn uncomfortable and adversarial after we have given them news they don't want to hear. Consider this scenario.

When Parent Pushback Gets Personal

Jennifer's first job as a principal was on an interim basis; she got the position after her predecessor retired unexpectedly in the middle of the year. The school was an excellent one, and parents and families were exceedingly welcoming. In Jennifer's first few days, she met hundreds of them and felt enveloped by a sense of helpful and supportive community. Among the families she met were Emilie, a 6th grader with an impish smile, and her mom.

Their first meeting took place in the car line, when Emilie bounded out of her mom's vehicle, held out a hand, and introduced herself: "I'm Emilie!" Leaving the car idling in line, Emilie's mother came up behind her and gave her own confident introduction. "We're going to get to know each other well, because you will be calling me daily," Emilie's mom said, laughing. "This one's a handful," she added, nodding toward her daughter, who gave a wide grin in return. "Yep, I'm a handful!" Emilie agreed.

Well, Jennifer thought, *if Emilie really is a handful, at least her mother will be supportive.* As it turned out, Emilie really was... and Emilie's mother was everything but.

Jennifer quickly learned that Emilie expressed herself—and any dissatisfaction she had—physically. She constantly pushed, shoved, and kicked her classmates. Her teacher had several behavior structures in place, but Emilie would watch for the moment the teacher looked away to go after one of her classmates. The previous principal had tried his best, but the teacher confided in Jennifer that he avoided getting that involved for fear of upsetting the parent. "I need your help," the teacher pleaded with Jennifer. She was out of ideas for helping Emilie and getting unrelenting pressure from other parents about Emilie's aggression toward her classmates. Jennifer promised to do everything she could.

But that same afternoon, Emilie had another incident, taking a classmate's pencil and breaking it over his head. When the classmate got upset, Emilie shoved him so hard the boy toppled to the floor, and when he tried to break his fall, he pierced his hand on the broken pencil shards scattered there. Later, with Jennifer in the principal's office, Emilie readily admitted to her actions. "That kid is annoying," she shrugged.

Jennifer filled out an Intend to Suspend form, spoke to the boy who'd been hurt, and then called the boy's mother. "Aren't you going to do something about Emilie?" the mother asked. "Isn't this considered bullying? This is the fourth time now, and my son doesn't feel safe in class." Jennifer offered reassurance that she was working through solutions. Then she called Emilie's mother. "Emilie will be suspended for one day," she told her. "Tomorrow, we will meet as a team to put a disciplinary plan in place."

Emilie's mother was furious. She started by accusing the principal of making the entire incident up, then shifted to insisting Jennifer didn't understand the developmental needs of children. She said Jennifer was abusing her power, was not appropriately trained, and hated kids. Taken aback and hurt, Jennifer acknowledged the parent's anger and repeated to Emilie's mother that she needed to come to school to pick up her daughter. She did . . . but within four hours, Emilie's mother had posted a screed on Facebook, emailed a three-page letter to every member of the Board of Education, and called the central office multiple times to try to get a meeting with the superintendent.

The campaign did not let up. Jennifer was just the interim principal but hoped to get the job permanently. Emilie's mom had other plans. When the permanent position interviews were being set up, she had her husband and sister volunteer to be on the parent interview committee. She spread falsehoods about Jennifer to anyone who would listen. An entire neighborhood of hundreds of families was hearing untrue accusations about the principal's character, and there didn't seem to be anything the principal could do about it.

When parents go after a principal—personally, professionally, and, worst of all, publicly—it can be devastating. Staying silent in the face of it is a very difficult thing to do, especially when parents' perceptions feel like judgments, unwarranted and unexpected. Attacks on our integrity, competence, and personality indicate the parent doesn't trust us, which, in turn, robs us of the ability to trust them. Being mistrusted leads to an unwillingness to trust.

Here's the point where I reveal that the "Jennifer" in this scenario is me, Jen. Back then, I followed the advice of a colleague and did not respond to this parent's attacks. I have since come to understand that silence—as stifling as it felt—really was my best choice. Had I tried to defend myself, it would have been just more fuel to the flame. Instead, I channeled my "feeling wronged" energy toward a response that would help Emilie, her classmates, and her teachers. As it turned out, this student and parent had enough of a reputation that no one in the school community thought less of me for suspending her. On the contrary, my decision to (finally) take action received a lot of silent applause. When our PBIS team met to discuss a plan for addressing Emilie's behavior, we were united in our advocacy for her. Our collective care, wisdom, and preparation were undeniable—even to Emilie's mother. Although she remained icy to me, she did accept the plan and went on to support the teachers and staff in implementation.

For a principal in a situation similar to this one, with hurt feelings and damaged trust, there are many possible response paths. Let's think about one that's unlikely to go well, one that would be workable, and one that's likely to have a positive outcome:

- *Bad response:* Consider a partnership with the parent an impossibility. Suspend the child for every infraction that could merit suspension. Tell the staff all about how the parent has mistreated you so that they will stand with you.
- *Good response:* Ask an assistant principal, counselor, or a district administrator to be the future point of contact with the parent. Be available to answer the parent's questions, but stay out of it as much as you can. Stand ready to be supportive if the parent turns on these colleagues as she turned on you.
- *Most effective response:* Continue to communicate as you would with any other parent. Be clear and honest in your interactions, using a professional and personable approach. Follow up any conversations with an email capturing your points and acknowledging her perspective as well. Copy members of the team to ensure everyone is on the same page and to protect yourself.

Dislike or disrespect from a parent always feels deflating. And it happens fairly often, because the principal is usually the one responsible for delivering news parents don't want to hear. I've struggled to make peace with this reality, and it helps when I remind myself there are usually hundreds of supportive parents, far more than the few who are not. I also discipline myself to control my own trusting behaviors. I build the pillars. I try to be trustworthy. And in spite of betrayals, I ask myself to always be someone who is willing to trust others.

Trust Killers with Parents

Before we dig into ways to be trustworthy and trust willing with parents, let's uncover some common ways principals might unintentionally compromise trust with parents.

Dismissing safety concerns

The top cause of parental anxiety and fear is concerns about safety. The trust pillars involved here are *professionalism* and *competence*. Unfortunately, fears about safety renew themselves; every time a news story shows schoolchildren in unsafe situations, parent worry spikes, and this worry cumulates over time. For principals, trying to reassure parents is both necessary and complicated, because there is an unspoken truth that is deeply uncomfortable: just as we can't guarantee a child will be safe going to a concert or the mall, we cannot promise parents their children will always be safe at school. We can, however, do our very, *very* best to create safe environments, both physically and emotionally.

For the purposes of this conversation, let's keep our focus on a school's physical safety. As all principals know, there is a tenuous balance between being open about safety plans and keeping details under wraps—after all, publishing a safety plan for full public access would compromise its components. We cannot tell a community about evacuation locations, about the where students would go if there were an intruder, or about systems and training provided to protect students from danger. Yet parents need to know that the school prioritizes safety just as they do, so principals might think about how to communicate basic facts about safety plans. For example, parents can be reassured that safety drills are conducted with regularity; that safety experts are called upon to advise and audit safety practices; and that the school has a tight working relationship with local law enforcement, fire/EMS organizations, and governmental regulators.

If there is a safety breach of some kind, principals should communicate what they know and when they know it. I once worked in a school across the street from a gas station that was robbed several times over the course of several years. Each time there was a robbery, we went into lockdown, and I worked closely with the police department's communications office to develop email and text communication that would reassure parents that their children were safe but not compromise the investigation. We signed our emails with both my name and that of the police chief to reassure parents we were in partnership with crime experts and that the lockdown would not be lifted until the suspect was in custody.

Weak communication

As noted earlier, communication is a throughline in themes about parent trust. The *clarity* trust pillar is compromised when parents lack accurate, thorough, and understandable information. To break that down further, let's think of how each could be a trust killer. First, sharing inaccurate or unverified information starts rumors and fuels anxiety. *Incomplete information* kills trust because in general, people will create a narrative if a reasonable one isn't provided. If principals share too little information, if the information feels cryptic, or if there are obvious omissions, parents will begin to fill in the holes with assumptions and rumors. Finally, if our communication relies too much on jargon and acronyms, if we don't proofread our communication for clarity, and if we don't have someone else put their eyes on our messages to ensure they make sense, the information may not be received as we intended.

Undisciplined behavior and appearance

I know a principal who readily admits his temper has undercut his efforts to appear trustworthy. Because he sometimes fails to contain his frustration or anxiety in emotionally fraught circumstances, he struggles to lead through tense situations. He is working on his responses, using Steven Hayes's Acceptance & Commitment Therapy (ACT) approach described in his books *A Liberated Mind* (2020) and *Get Out of Your Mind and Into Your Life* (2005).

This principal is far from alone. I know another principal, a natural introvert, who can come off as aloof or disengaged, and yet another one whose eyes involuntarily fill with tears whenever she is feeling very emotional. Principals are subject to scrutiny of their appearance, too: how they dress, how they wear their hair, the levels of authority and relatability they exude, and so on. Even if a principal is an extremely strong and capable leader, negative outward responses have the potential to erode trust in the eyes of parents.

Inconsistent student discipline

When different students are held to different standards of behavior, trust with their parents breaks down.

Many, many years ago, when I was a student, it was well known that athletes on the wrestling team, which was coached by the assistant principal's husband, were able to get away with almost anything. They skipped class, cussed, cheated, and were rude to other students—and they never got in trouble. Forty years later, I still remember the feeling of how unfair this was. My classmates and I talked about these inequities with our parents, and this was a factor in their distrust of the school's leadership.

These days, it is standard practice for schools to thoroughly analyze discipline data to spot trends and make sure that no student or group is unfairly targeted. This approach allows us to examine our biases in discipline decisions and fosters trust with parents, who depend on the school to treat their children equitably.

Devaluing parent priorities

"What is important to you?" This is actually a great question to ask parents. What *do* parents hope the school is doing for their child? What *do* they want their child to get out of the school experience?

We often assume parents want academic achievement, physical safety, and social-emotional growth, but there are other things that parents prioritize, too—some big and some small. On the big side, parents may identify maintaining discipline, embracing cutting-edge content or processes, or producing lots of graduates who go on to college as top priorities. On the small side, they may care about what school supplies to buy, what the bus routes will be, and what the drop-off and pickup procedures are. My personal belief is that parents will always prioritize their own child's experience, but they also want their child to be part of something that does not cause additional stress for the child, for them, or for the collective parent group.

Successful principals do not ignore or dismiss parent priorities; instead, they work to understand them.

Defensiveness

Some principals are staunchly defensive of particular systems or people and cannot see how misguided their defense might be. A principal might have rolled out a particular curricular resource that promised great results and refuse to admit that its real-life effects are modest at best. Or a principal might defend a teacher who is ineffective, unkind, or unorganized out of loyalty. Principal support of teachers is important if warranted, but ignoring contrary evidence isn't.

Limiting parent access

A principal friend of mind recently told me that during the COVID-19 pandemic, parents at his school were gracious and understanding about protocols put into place to keep students safe by limiting outside visitors. Afterward, though, some parents felt the school should revert to pre-pandemic business as usual, even if that meant abandoning security operations that proved to be helpful during the pandemic, such as new sign-in procedures, limited in-school parties and celebrations, and more oversight with parent volunteers. "This school has become like Fort Knox," one parent complained. "Only a few 'anointed ones' can get in."

While a school can't throw open the doors for anyone to come in any time, leaders damage trust with parents when access restrictions contribute to them feeling disconnected or isolated from the school. This goes double in the absence of events built on parent participation and family involvement.

Adopting a victim mentality

There is no disputing that being an educator is a difficult job, but I cringe whenever I overhear principals tell parents, explicitly or implicitly, that they are overworked or overwhelmed. It may be true, and parents may be empathetic, but there is a time and place for sharing our professional frustrations, and it's rarely when parents are around. They have their own stresses to manage! And given that few parents have the job security and vacation time many teachers have, it's best not to push their sympathy. Leaning on our *professionalism* trust pillar is the best way to keep away from what I call a "suffering contest."

Passing the disciplinary buck

At lunch not long ago, a friend of mine talked about her children's principal with what sounded like annoyance. She explained that the principal's regular newsletter usually contains a scolding aimed at unnamed subgroups of students. For example, he might write, "The students have been very loud in the lunchroom; please talk to your child about using softer voices in the cafeteria," or "We had an assembly this week, and I was very disappointed by the behavior of a select group of students; please review standard rules of public conduct with your kids," or "This week, a few students brought large bags of candy to school and caused a disruption in art class. We ask that you not allow your child to bring bags of candy."

There are two problems with these messages. It is unlikely that many parents will do "as requested" and speak to their child about these matters, even if their child is among those who exhibited the unacceptable behavior. As a behavior management strategy, it's a bad one. Second, just as the offending students may not receive the message, innocent ones will likely be implicated in offenses they haven't committed.

It is far better to address problems with the appropriate students in the moment rather than ask an undifferentiated mass of parents to intervene after the fact. They will have little idea how their child is involved and little power to do anything to change a situation they don't understand. They might even feel insulted by the implication they are to blame ("My child knows all about the standard rules of public conduct, thank you very much!").

Trust Pillars with Parents

Now that we have covered some common ways principals might damage trust with students' parents, let's look at the trust pillars they can build with this demographic.

It might surprise you to learn that a good relationship between a student's parents and their principal does have a positive association with academic performance. It's something like a trickle-down effect: if parents are connected and involved in their child's school, this engagement improves teacher perception of parents, and a positive teacher perception of parents is positively associated with student achievement (Gordon & Louis, 2009).

> Higher parent engagement is associated with higher student achievement.

There are all kinds of ways a principal can build trusting relationships with parents by being intentionally trustworthy. In almost all of the examples I'm about to share, we will focus on how the principal interacts with parents; however, these principal-parent interactions can also serve as models for teachers' interactions with parents. They are just as effective in bolstering teachers' trustworthiness as they are a principal's.

Hearing what's being said

When a parent is talking about their child, they want to be heard. As educators, we know that a parent's perspective on a situation can be very illuminating, whether the discussion is positive (e.g., a celebration of a student's progress or achievement) or negative (e.g., a failure to follow the rules, struggles with academic content). Over the years, I am certain that I missed many trust-building opportunities in rushed-through parent phone calls. Experience has taught me to slow down and listen more closely when a parent is sharing their thoughts. When they are less forthcoming, I've learned to ask, "Can you tell me what you're thinking right now?" and "Is there anything you'd like me to know?" I try to listen carefully to understand more exactly what the parent needs from me—more information? A repeat of the details? A place to share their concerns? Specific actions?

Not long ago, a teacher I know met with a parent who was questioning results from a recent standardized test. The test score was quite a bit lower than the parent had expected, and she seemed unable to get out of a cycle of disbelief, blame, and defensiveness. The teacher reminded her this was actually a low-stakes test and then asked her, "Can you tell me what has you the most concerned?" The parent admitted to worrying that her child was a terrible test-taker. What if poor results now would be mirrored in high-stakes tests, thereby affecting his options for college? The teacher was able to reassure her that this one test was not an indication of the student's long-range future. This story is a good reminder that students benefit when we prompt and listen for useful input during parent-teacher conversations and that it's important to build time into each conference for this kind of focused listening.

Being responsive and accountable

When something goes sideways in a school, the principal's willingness to accept responsibility and ability to explain and execute a reasonable response is a significant reassurance to parents. Making smart, visible changes in response to conflicts or challenges tells parents that you can be trusted to do what you say you will do and that your chosen plan is a good one.

One of my colleagues recently hosted a parent event in the evening. Her guess at how many parents would attend was way off, and the big crowd quickly threatened to overwhelm the space. She was able to open up some additional rooms, and the evening ended reasonably well, but in her newsletter communication that week, she admitted the event was too crowded and promised that when she hosted it again next year, she'd do two things differently: make sure to have extra staff available and prepare additional areas of the building to manage the influx of attendees. And that's exactly what she did.

Engaging in frequent, relevant communication

As recently mentioned, there are many ways to make communication a foundational pillar of trust for your school. As a matter of fact, strong, regular communication is such an effective trust builder that it's worth taking a closer look at several of the components involved:

- *Training and empowering staff.* Teachers who communicate frequently and thoroughly will help parents not only know what to expect, know, and understand about their child's classroom, but also develop a deeper sense of trust in the principal's leadership and the school in general. As an added bonus, when teachers communicate well, it reduces the number of phone calls parents might need to place with the main office to clear up confusing information.

- *Archiving communication for easy access.* Like most parents, I often read communication from my child's school when it comes home, but when I actually need to reference or access the information later, it seems to take forever to find it again. I am always appreciative when school provides a central place to access past communication. A website or newsletter platform is useful for this purpose.
- *Getting to know students.* Communicating with parents is infinitely easier when we know a little something about their children. Obviously, this is quite a bit easier in small schools, but even in larger schools, principals knowing a student by name and having a few bits of information about them makes individual conversations with parents much better. Even something as simple as "I noticed Kelsie has a new haircut!" or "I had a great conversation with Quinn yesterday!" will reassure parents that the principal notices and cares about their children.
- *Communicating directly with individual parents.* Phone calls, car line conversations, and emails to individual parents about their child are all opportunities to connect on an individual basis. The direct approach is best for behavior issues, too; as noted earlier, "select group" behavior issues should be handled individually and promptly, not in undifferentiated, all-school communications.
- *Compiling and sending mass communications on a predictable schedule.* Communications about all-school events, updates on classroom activities, and overall general messages can go out to the entire school community. But here's a caution that always sending out information as it comes in, or as schedules are set, will create communication fatigue; if parents are getting daily messages or even messages several times a week, it won't be long before they start to overlook or delete them. I've found that parents appreciate it when principals compile all information into a regular, once-a-week email and send outliers (via text, if possible) only when there is an emergency.
- *Tailoring your communication.* When something affects only one subgroup of students (e.g., an update on a grade-level field trip or a late bus), it helps to communicate only with the affected

families. If a parent of a sophomore receives emails that say, "For freshmen parents," it just desensitizes them to school communication; far better to send information only to the recipients who need it.

Being present and engaged at school events

Families love seeing principals at events, and they love seeing the principal's active participation at these events even more. Whether it's an elementary music show, a middle school band concert, or a high school athletic contest, a principal's attendance demonstrates dedication and commitment to the school's students. It can also help build one-on-one relationships between the principal and the parents they meet at these events.

Following through

Parents appreciate follow-through from principals. This might be calling a parent as soon as possible after a behavior investigation, checking in after a complicated IEP meeting, or sticking to promises made during an event or presentation. If we say, for example, "After tonight's presentation, I'll include the slide deck in my newsletter so you can go back and reference the main points I've made," parents appreciate seeing the slide deck in the next newsletter.

Managing hard conversations with tact and calm

Having difficult conversations with parents is part of a principal's job. How we handle these conversations will be interpreted and shared with others—at the pool, at a neighborhood block party, online—and a trust pillar will be either reinforced or broken. There are layers of nuance to consider when managing difficult conversations. Here are a few things to keep in mind:

- *Consider how parents are feeling.* Speaking with a principal about a child is difficult; it feels tense, scary, and full of anxiety. The principal can alleviate some of those feelings by expressly identifying them ("I know this must feel confusing and scary") or, even better, by inviting the parent to share what is going on in their minds ("Would you like to share how you're feeling about this conversation?"). The principal has an enormous capacity to make people feel heard, to preserve their dignity, and to provide empathy and compassion. These opportunities remind me of some wise words usually attributed to Maya Angelou: "People will forget what you said, people will forget what you did, but people will never forget how you made them feel."

- *Remember your intended outcome.* When having hard conversations, I try to stay focused on an intentional path toward a positive outcome. What do I need to say to the parent? How might I say it to get to an outcome in which I say the necessary things but also remain a partner and teammate with them?

- *Identify the parent's hoped-for outcome.* You may have an idea of how the conversation should go, only to find the parent has a completely different game plan. Again, honest and open dialogue can help bridge any gaps. You might ask, "What do you hope to gain from this conversation?" If their stated goal is different from yours, follow up with more questions: "Do you understand what I'm hoping to get out of our meeting today? Is there any way we can come together to support the student, even though our intended outcomes differ?"

- *Recognize power dynamics and bias.* Few of us enjoy losing, and this facet of human nature can get in the way of solution finding. During conversations with parents, keep an eye out for expressions and vocal tones that suggest the parent sees the exchange as something to be "won," and modify your words and manner in a way that emphasizes cooperation. Look, too, for signs a parent assumes you will "win" simply because you, as principal, hold a type of power. It's important to reinforce the idea that you are a fair and open listener and a partner in serving their child's best interests. Ask parents what outcome they're hoping for. Get their ideas. Stress that you're there to work with them to find a solution that will suit and serve everyone. Similarly, any bias in the situation, on your part or on the part of a parent, might need to be addressed so it doesn't become a point of contention later.

- *Be on the lookout for conversation stoppers.* If a parent gets defensive, hostile, passive-aggressive, or heavily emotional, I consider whether it's enough of a problem to stop the conversation. When we are past the point of productivity, I might ask for a pause in the dialogue so everyone can take a break or get a drink of water. I might also stop the meeting and ask for a time to reconvene, perhaps with additional support in the room—a school counselor, a teacher, an expert in behavior, or whomever might help us come to a resolution.

- *Balance empathy with professionalism.* I'll never forget the time I met with a parent whose child had assaulted and injured a classmate. The mother was combative herself, and as we spoke, she told me she was going through her third divorce, was involved in an employment dispute, and was at risk of losing custody of her two younger children. The challenges she was facing explained a lot about her son's behaviors. Feeling terribly sorry for her, I reached for her hand and said, "You must be in such pain. This is a lot to be going through." She snatched her hand away, snapping, "I don't need your pity." I was stung, but I knew she was right. She didn't need my pity; she needed me to help her son through a difficult time. I straightened up, apologized, and asked for her input in making a plan for his return to school.

Learning and honoring each student's story

Taking time to know a little something about each student reassures parents that their child is in good hands. Yes, this can be difficult in large schools, but in those cases, a team of assistants can help carry the responsibility of connecting with and learning about students.

I know many principals who aren't shy about taking notes. Personally, I have learned that if I want to remember a student's name, I either need to hear the name three times or I need to connect the student and their name to some kind of memorable anecdote. So, I combine these methods: I get a student's name and ask them to tell me something about themselves. Next, I go back a couple times to ask for more details, saying the student's name aloud each time. Then, when I meet their parents, I can easily pull information from my own mental database and show the parents that I care about their child and know a little bit about them.

If I know a student or family has dealt with trauma or difficulty, I try to honor the journey their lives have taken. My goal is to be the kind of person that both students and their parents consider a trusted supporter.

Showing Parents You Are Trust Willing

Now that we've covered ways principals can be trustworthy with parents, let's look at the other side of the equation: ways principals might demonstrate that they are willing to trust parents, too. Proceeding from the conversation in Chapter 2, giving parents chances to make decisions, elevating their voices, and treating them as partners are all great starting points. Now, I'd like to expand on these ideas and mention a few others.

Prioritize the parent-teacher relationship

It's important to remember that the relationship students have with their teachers is the most important factor in school-family partnerships. When students (and parents) trust in their teachers, there's often a halo effect on the administration as well. I am honored when parents trust the school—and me!—as a direct result of the trust they have with their child's teacher.

For a principal, it is an act of faith to let teachers foster relationships with students and parents. It's intentional faith, though, because we have a tremendous role in establishing an overall trusting culture that supports success. Principals really don't need to intervene unless there is something wrong or there is a difference of opinion that affects or compromises a child's experience.

Empower parent leadership

The connections parents have with their child's school are reinforced when parents have some decision-making power.

I once talked with a principal whose PTO wanted to make some fundamental changes to a long-standing event in the school. The event had never been the principal's responsibility, but for some reason he was resistant to letting the parents make change. "Why not?" I asked him. "Why do you care?" It was a serious question. Why *would* the principal care about a positive event run by his parents? Well, the principal said, he was worried the changes wouldn't be well received—would ruin the event—and he'd be the one held responsible. He also worried it would set a precedent in which parents just made sweeping changes, willy-nilly.

"Are you resisting an opportunity to let them lead, based solely on hypothetical what-ifs?" I asked him.

When he admitted that it might be true, I encouraged him to let it go. "It's an opportunity for them to lead, to have agency, to feel heard," I said. "Let them."

The principal was able to do just that, though he did establish guardrails by clearly articulating non-negotiables—specifics he didn't feel should change—such as an improvement in security protocols for the event. He also requested he be invited to participate in conversations to ensure he was in the loop with the proposed changes and could step in if there was anything he thought would result in a problem.

Identify key communicators

Many districts create specific parent groups to help communicate with the larger community. In my district, this group is called "key communicators." It comes together monthly or bi-monthly to share what is happening in the school district, both good and bad. Those parents are then asked to help share good news, set the record straight on social media if a post or comments go sideways, dispel inaccurate rumors in the community, and so on.

Key communicators are both the bringers and receivers of important information. They create an opportunity for deliberate distribution of facts and address community misunderstandings in intention and focus. In my experience, having this group is very effective, though it is worth mentioning that members sometimes report other parents feel resentful that they, too, cannot participate. In those cases, I remind them that the group is always evolving and growing, and as group members "graduate out," we open up to volunteers who are willing to fill any vacancies.

Use social media to your advantage

Most school administrators are frustrated by social media because of the residual effects it has on students, its tendency to host inaccurate information, and the inevitable perpetuation of rumors. But social media isn't going away, and it is increasingly a source of news and information for parents and students. That's why, in an example of "if you can't lick 'em, join 'em," I believe embracing social media as a communication tool can serve as a trust pillar and drown out some of the damaging social media that's out there.

Your goal should be to have a social media presence that can serve as a positive tool for the school. If, for example, a principal creates a private Facebook page, it's easy to limit members to only parents and staff members. Posts can come from the school or only with approval from the social media manager, ensuring accurate, up-to-date information along with celebrations and photographs. It can also be the one point of information, explanations, and updates. If parents post a comment that is actually a question pertinent only to their child, the social media manager can simply avoid approving the post and instead give the parent a call with the appropriately individualized answer.

The tips offered in this chapter apply to school leaders who are looking for ways to build and preserve trust with critical members of their communities. Of course, even with all the best intentions, principals will undoubtedly still encounter parents who disparage their efforts and remain skeptical—not only of the principal but often of the teachers and staff, too. Some parents just don't trust school. The origins of this may trace back years to their own student experiences, or it may be that recent events related to their own children have left them upset and hurt. I've had a few of those experiences myself as a mother raising my own children, and when they happen, I have to remind myself that it's not fair to paint an entire staff or school with a distrust brush because of any one thing that felt especially wrong or unfair. It's easy for me to catch myself, though, because I work in schools every day and see principals and teachers whose intentions are truly and unwaveringly positive. Imagine how difficult it is for parents to do so when they don't get a firsthand view of the positive, hardworking, dedicated staff members who work with children every day.

In the end, our power comes in doing our best to build trust pillars. We can deliberately and frequently think about how a child's experience translates into a parent's foundational trust and do our best to preserve it.

Trust with Students

Because it's usually the principal or an assistant principal who administers consequences when a student has made a poor choice, the dynamic between the principal and students can be an uneasy one. Many principals who work hard to connect with students are up against the idea, sometimes advanced by parents at home, that they are the enemy and not to be trusted.

This is a perspective I understand. As an elementary student in the late 1970s, I thought my own principal (I'll call him Mr. Moore) had just one job: to sit in his office and wait for a chance to use his paddle. All of us knew how it went: Mr. Moore would begin by asking you why you had been sent to his office. He'd listen to your explanation, then ask how many whacks of the paddle you thought you deserved. Whatever number he was given, he would invariably double or triple. "If Mr. Moore asks you how many whacks, *just say one*," we advised one another. If the student in his office was a girl, Mr. Moore called in his secretary as a witness. She would stand there miserably, flinching at each contact between paddle and child. Looking back, I don't know what parents or teachers thought of Mr. Moore, but I assume they considered him to be doing his job—carrying out the duties expected of a school principal in the 1970s. From the perspective of students, though, Mr. Moore was a hated man.

Fortunately, the profession has evolved such that principals now strive to build constructive relationships with students and families, collaborate in mutual advocacy of a student's growth, and avoid causing pain. This is harder than it sounds, especially when students are predisposed to view the principal with doubt and distrust. But there is a way to be both an advocate for student growth and a respected figure who can, and will, say and do the difficult work necessary to support students.

As a principal, I took pride in having good relationships with students, but my track record is not perfect. Every few years, there would be a student or two who made me want to scream because despite all my efforts, despite my extensive bag of tricks, they kept making poor choices, kept getting themselves in frustrating situations, showed mind-boggling disrespect, and seemed uninterested in my efforts to help them. Having worked with students of all ages, I have found it generally easier to build trusting relationships with elementary students than with middle and high school students. It might be a factor of adolescence. When teens and tweens process events with their friends, they sometimes need to find a scapegoat, and that scapegoat is often the principal.

A Closer Look at Fractured Trust with Students

Once again, let's start with a scenario to consider. This time, it's an instance of fractured trust between a principal and a student. We'll consider what the principal might do in response, and then we'll dive into ways a principal might improve and increase reciprocal trust.

Caught Off Guard

Deacon, an experienced and knowledgeable principal, had what he thought was a typical interaction with a student. The boy's name was Alex, and he had been caught selling vape pens while he was supposed to be in physical education class. Deacon looked into the incident, talked with the parties involved and some witnesses, then suspended the student. Alex's parents demanded a meeting, which Deacon spent listening to accusations that he had said and done things he had not done and would not *dream* of doing. But some of the things they referenced did sound vaguely familiar. It slowly dawned on him that these parents were quoting isolated phrases he'd used during his investigation and reinserting them out of context in a way that made it seem he was fabricating the situation.

When Deacon pushed back with a correction, Alex's parents announced, rather triumphantly, that they had proof. Alex had recorded the conversation he'd had with Deacon. The school was in a one-party consent state. The parents argued that because the person who'd made the recording (their son, the student) had "consented," there had been no need to get consent from the other party (the principal, Deacon). That Deacon didn't know he was being recorded was, in legal terms, irrelevant.

Deacon was confident he had not said or done anything inappropriate, inaccurate, or unprofessional, so he invited the parents to play the recording in its entirety and explained they had the right to appeal the suspension. Perhaps because they knew nothing on the recording would implicate the principal in any way, the parents backed off and relented, albeit angrily, to the suspension. Still, Deacon was left feeling betrayed. "I wish I had known Alex was recording me," he told me. "Now when I'm speaking with students, I'm wondering if I can trust them. Will they take my words out of context or splice them together to make our conversations into something different than they were? It makes me feel like I shouldn't talk to students at all."

Deacon's feelings of betrayal are understandable; however, the solution *isn't* to stop talking to students. Principals in Deacon's situation need to develop an approach based on being more careful with their words. I have long advised principals, "Never say anything to a student—or anyone, for that matter—that you wouldn't want on the front page of the newspaper." In today's digital age, it's worth adding, "And never say anything you wouldn't want played back to you."

In some ways, the possibility of being recorded can serve as a comfort for principals. Long before students had such limitless recording capabilities, I could count on some who'd visited my office to tell their parents that I'd "yelled" or "screamed" at them. Inevitably, the parents would call to reprimand me for my tone—sometimes, I suspected, in an attempt to make the problem about me, not their child, and to get me to reverse course or relax or overturn a consequence. I hated these accusations. I was not a yeller, and I never screamed; it wasn't in my nature. When parents accused me of doing so, I would object. "Yes, I was stern and authoritative," I'd say, "but I can promise you I did *not* yell at your child." I hated the defensive tone of my voice during these times, hated that I had to defend myself. When denying the parent's accusations, I was acutely aware that I was creating tension between the child's word and that child's parents. Many times, I actually *wished* for a recording to prove how I'd interacted, to show I wasn't the person they were making me out to be, and to turn it into a teachable moment between a child, a parent, and the school.

I learned, as Deacon should, that even with hurt feelings and damaged trust, there are many approaches a principal might take in response to this kind of situation. Let's think about potential ways Deacon might respond—one unlikely to go well, one that would probably be workable, and one that is most likely to produce a positive outcome:

- *Bad response:* Look forward to the next time this student is sent to the office, and when he is, insist he leave his phone outside. Double down on the consequences for rule infringements; after all, this is a dishonest and manipulative student, right?
- *Good response:* In an effort to be completely open and honest, invest in a recording system. When students are in your office, announce an intent to record the conversation. Alternatively, always have a second person (e.g., an assistant principal, a counselor, a teacher) in the room during conversations with students.

- *Most effective response:* Embrace the mindset shift that every conversation—not just with students but also with parents, teachers, and other colleagues—is being recorded. Work on speaking from fact, not emotion, and strive to be polite, professional, and firm.

I know some of you may be thinking, *Sure, principals can take precautions and shift mindsets, but isn't there always a chance students will twist our words, misinterpret our tone, or spread falsehoods that can threaten our professional reputations?* Yes, there is always that chance, but I want to repeat a point from earlier chapters: there is no point in trying to control what others say and do about you. You're likely to do better work when you're not living on edge. Let others talk if they must. Focus on controlling what you can—yourself, the ways you express trust in others, and the ways you show yourself worthy of others' trust.

And how does that look in practice? As a first step, principals can think about what might be reinforcing students' predispositions to mistrust them. We can reflect on both our own actions and those of teachers and staff to see if there are ways we might be unintentionally undermining trust with students.

> Respond to students with thought, care, and simplicity. As soon as possible after a discipline-focused encounter, shift the focus back to academic content.

Trust Killers with Students

Students are more likely to trust a school—its teachers, its principal, its culture—if they know that they, their friends, and their family members will always be treated with dignity and respect. It's the responsibility of school leadership to foster and maintain a culture like this.

Making a personal commitment to be kind and respectful to students is the easy part. Ideally, all staff members should strive for kindness and acceptance all the time, no matter who the child is and no matter what behavior they are displaying. Over the years, I have had to sit down with a few staff members and point out the reputation they'd built as intolerant of particular subsets of students—those from marginalized or minority populations, students who are not compliant, those who struggle with classroom work or expectations, or even students who are not "popular." I once pursued formal discipline for a teacher who treated English learners as incompetent, unintelligent, or deaf. She would raise her voice and speak in an embarrassingly slow tone. I watched these students cringe and shrink in their seats when they were in her presence, afraid that if they caught her eye, she'd treat them like toddlers. I warned this teacher multiple times about these microaggressions, which were having a negative impact on our entire school culture. I stressed how important it was for students to know their teachers would treat them with dignity. Formal disciplinary action was my last resort. Yes, the teacher was furious. Yes, she bad-mouthed me to her colleagues. But I can't say I was upset to find out she was going around asking them if they could *believe* I had disciplined her for being rude to students. I *wanted* them to believe it! I wanted every staff member to know they would be held to a standard of helpful, positive, honorable interactions with every single student.

Effective teachers are confident in students' ability to learn; those same students trust their teachers will work for them and encourage their growth. In other words, teachers "cannot educate students in whom they have no confidence, and students cannot learn from teachers whom they do not trust. These reciprocal beliefs, when implemented together, result in respect manifested as esteem for teachers by students and esteem for students by teachers" (Willie, 2000, p. 255). Students who are confident in themselves perform better in school and are also more likely to attempt challenging learning activities (Moneva & Tribunalo, 2020).

The same concept applies to interactions between peers. If a school's culture is one in which physical incidents or verbal attacks are not properly investigated

High levels of trust, confidence, and reciprocal esteem between students and their peers and between students and their teachers improve student achievement.

and addressed, it's a sure bet there are students in the building who feel it is not a safe environment. How students are treated by their classmates has a significant impact on their achievement (Burke & Sass, 2013).

Let's consider a few more behaviors that are sure to break trust between students and staff.

Public embarrassment

No one likes to be called out, shamed, or humiliated. When the principal, teachers, or peers push a student to stand out, stand alone, and suffer judgment, the embarrassment they feel can be something they carry for years. In an example that I hope no one still sees today, I remember when teachers would have students trade-and-grade, then read their scores aloud for the teacher to record in the grade book. Any teacher-initiated situation that embarrasses a student is a situation likely to damage trust.

Favoritism

There was a teacher at the school my nieces attended who seemed to be trying to re-live her own teenage years. She gravitated to a certain "popular" group of girls, offering them extra study hall time with her, routinely excusing them from homework, and huddling with them in the hall. She opened her classroom to weekly invite-only lunches, during which she encouraged her favorites to "spill the tea" about their classmates. While this is a more blatant example of favoritism, it's an all too common problem. Some principals and teachers unintentionally favor certain subgroups—athletes, academically gifted students, behaviorally compliant ones, girls, or boys. Students who are the recipients of this favoritism often notice it and feel uncomfortable, and for students outside the favoritism circle, it is difficult, if not impossible, to trust in these teachers' goodwill.

Lack of due process

"Can I *please* just tell you what happened?" When students say this in a discipline situation, they're telling you they don't feel heard. Students need to trust that they will be given a chance to tell their side of the story. Even when knowing their "side" won't change what happened or the consequences of it, a student's side always matters because the *student* always matters. Failure to guarantee due process sends the opposite message.

The Supreme Court's 1975 *Goss v. Lopez* decision confirmed students' right to due process before being suspended from school. But independent of legality, it's clear that a principal who fails to ask questions and listen when called to investigate behavioral issues is communicating "I don't care what you think" and "You do not matter." Trust is impossible in an atmosphere like that.

Ambiguous or arbitrary decisions

When decisions feel ambiguous or arbitrary, it's hard to settle into a mindset of trust. Knowing why things happen as they do—why the schedule is arranged as it is, why there will be this consequence for that negative behavior, why attendance and tardiness matter, why we can or should not do and say certain things—won't make students happy, necessarily, but it does reassure them that decisions are made with thought and reason. I've found that policies, practices, and protocols linked to fairness and order, which students value highly, are especially reassuring.

Exclusivity

While there is value in "Student of the Month" and "Superstar Student" awards and benefits to positive behavior management systems, they come at a cost. Award programs, which begin as young as preschool and continue through high school, often honor "types"—scholars, athletes, or students to whom school comes naturally. The same top performers tend to be recognized year after year. There are many children with strong grades who are never in trouble and consistently earn positive reports from teachers who never receive a special recognition. Some might justify this with the same kind of "meritocracy" argument that sniffs at the idea of "everybody getting a trophy." Yet I wonder why *every* kid can't be recognized for the unique gifts they have. When we "leave out" the same students year after year, we teach them that only certain types of students are valued within the school setting. I've known schools to develop a quick data system that ensures all students get some sort of recognition over the course of the year, even if it is just an acknowledgment of effort.

Disrespect

Young people are full of ideas: personal initiatives, policies they want revised, clubs they want to start, schedule changes they'd like to see... the list goes on. Students with ideas like this should be acknowledged, not ignored. It's a matter of respect.

I am reminded of a time, years ago, when a group of 6th grade students approached me with an idea to start a school newspaper. I didn't want to crush their initiative, but I also didn't think we had the resources to oversee a paper. So I took the easy way out, which was to push their written proposal around on my desk for several months. One morning, walking the halls before class started, I saw the students distributing a newspaper they'd made on their own—a homemade effort, visually clunky with photocopied "articles" pasted on spiral-bound notebook paper and stapled together with one of those tiny staplers. They had done what they could to create a newspaper on their own. Unfortunately, many of their classmates were dismissive or mocking. I felt terrible; their passion for the project was real, and it must have seemed to them as though I just didn't care. Had I heard them out, I could have offered some guidance or resources to help make it a success. I even could have told them, "No, not now," and offered a reason. But my response—ignoring them—was worse because it was fundamentally disrespectful.

Overstepping

Principals are accustomed to giving their all, and this can extend to trying to control situations that might not be controllable. Efforts to prevent one outcome may lead to a less desirable outcome or, worse, be a long-term trust killer for the way they compromise the *competence* trust pillar.

As an example, a few years ago, students in a county near mine organized a peaceful walkout to protest gun violence. Using social media, they mobilized peers from all four high schools in the area. The principals at two of these schools responded by trying to shut down the planned action; there would be no protest at their schools! At the other two schools, the principals collaborated on a plan. They met with student leaders and discussed the best way to make an impact without triggering disruptions. They led conversations about how dissenters might express their contrary opinions or organize their own protest, creating space for critical thinking and individual viewpoints. It was all thoughtfully arranged, and the walkout turned out to be a beautifully calm and respectful event.

Not so at the other two schools. Being shut down so quickly inflamed the students. They looked into their district policies—which *did*, in fact, allow for a walkout, in alignment with student constitutional rights to assemble peaceably to publicly express their ideas and opinions. These students continued to plan their protest in whispers, without the knowledge of school officials. Sensing an opportunity for drama and resistance, more and more students joined the effort. In the end, the two principals who'd earlier denied the students their request faced a very large group of students walking out. It was a loud and confusing situation, and it led to unmanageable discipline situations, the arrival of news crews, and even calls from the ACLU. This was a case of broken trust escalating into something much bigger than it needed to be—and more damaging.

This list of trust-killing behaviors is reassuring in an important way: these actions are usually avoidable. Simply saying yes more often to students' ideas and initiatives will go a long way toward building trust and mutual respect within a school. Let's shift our mindsets to think of other ways principals can develop trust pillars with their students and encourage teachers to do the same.

Trust Pillars with Students

In a world that is unpredictable and chaotic, schools should be a place of predictability and calm. I always want students to know they can count on us—teachers, principals, and staff. Unfortunately, some of our students might have very little they can trust, so the adults at school are the primary role models they have for seeing how trust can be built, nourished, and maintained.

So what can a principal do to ensure this happens? What makes for a trustworthy school environment? As with the items we discussed as trust killers, there are two aspects to consider. The first is how the principal acts and behaves, and the second is the extent to which the teachers and staff follow the principal's model for engaging with students. After all, every staff member should be trustworthy. Students who are in classrooms in which they trust their teachers as leaders and figures of authority are more likely to engage in academic tasks and less likely to lose instructional time due to disruptive discipline referrals (Gregory & Ripski, 2008).

> When students trust their teachers, behavior referrals are lowered and instructional interruptions are lessened, which increases students' engagement in academic work.

Showing commitment

Building trust with students means they need to know you're all in. You're "there for it," as students like to say. The trust pillar at work here is *availability*, and it can take many forms. Here are a few:

- Asking questions about what students are learning and what they like about school
- Being in the hallways during class change
- Referring students to the staff person who can help
- Showing students that, like them, you value extracurriculars and elective coursework such as art, music, physical education, library, and technology classes
- Being present during arrival and dismissal—especially in lousy weather
- Sitting with a young student whose parents are running late with pickup
- Eating lunch with groups of students in the cafeteria

Being authentic

Who are you as a human being? What matters to you, professionally and personally? Do you feel comfortable letting students see your fun side, your silly side, your imperfect side? I'm not suggesting you become someone you're not; if you are a serious type without a strong silly side, that's also OK! The point is that students who you allow to see you as a human being will be more apt to trust you.

When I provide professional development to new principals, I get a good laugh every time I tell them about the "dress code" I adopted during my first year as an administrator. I thought I had to be a strict, emotionless schoolmarm type, so I went to a well-known ladies' clothing store and bought a new wardrobe of professional clothes: black and brown blazers, sensible heels, lots of tweed. It was like playing dress-up every day. It took me a couple of years to recognize how uncomfortable I was. I had no business dressing like that—it wasn't me. I was covering my insecurities in a suit, assuming formal business attire would lend me an authority I didn't feel. With confidence and time, my clothes have come to better reflect who I am—certainly professional but definitely more relaxed and casual. I also do silly things with my presentation: dressing up in costume for special occasions, wearing athletic clothes for the annual walk-a-thon, putting on an entire chef outfit to grill hot dogs on Field Day. This is not to say everyone should be like me—on the contrary, no one should be like *me*, because every principal should just be who *they* are. If we're authentic, we'll be relatable. It's easier to trust someone who is relatable.

When you're thinking about how you might show your school community a more relaxed side of yourself, think about *professionalism* and *vulnerability*. I've seen principals rapping at assemblies. Dancing in the pickup line. Embracing the pop culture students love. Making YouTube videos of books through read-alouds. Some—not me, but some!—climb enthusiastically into dunk tanks and are perfectly willing to be duct-taped to a wall for fundraising purposes. The point is, you build a trust pillar when you have the confidence to be the whole person you are.

Engaging sincerely

I once had a group of students tell me their principal attended their musical shows but spent the entire time hanging in the back of the auditorium, scrolling through social media on his phone. I understand why principals might do this, and I confess I have done it myself. Extending professional "on time" into evening events can be exhausting, and it's normal to doubt the return on investment. The return *will* come, though, if the engagement is authentic. Students notice a principal's presence—and they will appreciate it if they see your interest is sincere.

Here is the formula that worked for me. For big annual events, such as the winter art show or spring orchestra concert, I committed to complete, phone-off engagement. But at recurring events, such as sports competitions or stage performances with multiple-night runs, I would make sure I was 100 percent visible and engaged at the beginning and end of the event, when crowds were coming and going. During the game or show, though, I might slip out to my office to get a few things done.

The natural effect of authentic engagement at events is greater connection with students, their parents, and their friends. I am someone who struggles to remember student names unless or until I have connected with them in a memorable way. If I see Amira delivering a speech at a student council session, if I see Kamir hitting a half-court basket, or if I chat with Donneta after the orchestra performance, I will remember their names thereafter and I will have something to talk about with them. Authentic engagement helps a principal to understand students' experiences, celebrate their successes, compliment them for their hard work, note important milestones when they come up, and so much more.

Here are some additional ways to engage sincerely:

- *Participate in field trips.* If your schedule allows for it, join in the fun of field trips. Even if I didn't have the hours to give to an all-day event, I would try to break away from school for an hour or two to drive to the site of the field trip and say hello. I also attended out-of-state field trips, leaving a member of the admin team "back home" and in charge. These trips are a lot, but they are also immeasurably rewarding, especially in terms of getting to know students and letting them know you.
- *Make your time with students immersive.* Don't just watch what's going on with students in a classroom—live the experience with

them. Instead of focusing on an observation checklist, sit down and attempt the math problem. Instead of walking through the cafeteria, take a turn standing in the cafeteria line. Walk alongside students during class changes and join them out in the cold for winter recess. If you're a high school principal, spend time in the parking lot when students arrive in the morning.
- *Stop by club and activity meetings.* Holding student council meetings, working on the yearbook, decorating for a dance, organizing the graphics for an upcoming newspaper—any time students gather together in the building is an opportunity to say hello, offer your support, and demonstrate your commitment.
- *Spend time in study areas.* If there are particular study spots in your school, such as an open learning space, a library, or furnished nooks, set up your laptop and join in the studying, reading, or group work.
- *Play.* If physically able, jump into staff-student tournaments. Join a game in the Gaga Pit. In physical education class, take part in a quick game of badminton. Go to a chess club meeting and challenge a student to a match.
- *Volunteer.* Show up and help out. Clean. Organize. Once when our cafeteria was down several employees, I spent a week of lunch periods serving food on the line. It was fantastic—a fun change of pace, for one thing, but also a chance to speak to students by name and enjoy their expressions when they saw their principal scooping mashed potatoes onto their plates.

Being clear and honest in all communications

Communicating directly with students increases the odds that your messages will be understood. Many principals do this through regular "town hall" meetings, in student leadership groups, over public address systems, and at large events. When problems arise, gathering a group of student leaders to talk through challenges and propose solutions helps them know the rationale behind the school's various systems and protocols. In other words, students feel more secure when they understand why things are the way they are. What's more, principals get a firsthand look at how their decisions affect their most important constituents: the students themselves.

As an example, a group of students approached a principal colleague of mine, frustrated by the lack of choices in the cafeteria. The principal connected with a social sciences teacher, who turned the question into a standard-linked, project-based-learning opportunity to identify the federal guidelines driving decisions about food choices. The students embraced the research. They learned how complicated it is to order, stock, and serve food that meets the set dietary guidelines. They discovered the difficulty in providing a wide array of food choices when every choice must meet the federal criteria and be something that's possible to order, store, prepare, and serve on a large scale, given the kitchen space and staffing conditions. This more comprehensive understanding of what goes into feeding a whole school for a whole school year was illuminating on its own, but it also solidified my principal colleague in these students' eyes as a trustworthy and respected straightshooter. And yes, this did quiet their complaints about the cafeteria menu.

> Direct engagement with students increases a school leader's sense of accountability.

Being consistent with student discipline

One of the least enjoyable parts of school leadership is managing conflict, discipline, and negative student interactions. Approaching these difficult situations with consistency and an eye to equity is a valuable trust pillar. When I advocate for *consistency*, I mean leadership must thoroughly investigate all student behavior incidents, follow a standard disciplinary process, and communicate with staff and parents in a sequential and thorough way. For example, a first-time infraction for one student should result in a similar consequence for any other student with a first-time infraction. However, an equitable approach might mean one of those students receives more pointed follow-up monitoring or support based on their individual needs.

Consistent student discipline does not mean it's uniform or inflexible. Recognizing that mandating all students receive the same consequence when they misstep is too simplistic an approach to be effective, many districts explicitly allow for principal discretion. In my district, principals code student behaviors with one of about 25 identifiers. Most come with a range of responses leading to a discipline ladder, with increasingly intense consequences for repeated violations. A couple, though, such as the descriptor "general misconduct," allows the principal full discretion on the consequence. This allows for important differentiation and an opportunity to build pillars of trust with students, based on the intricacies, antecedents, and response of those involved.

Being consistent with policy enforcement

Similarly, students will find their school, teachers, and principals more trustworthy if policies are enforced consistently. As we all know, this is easier said than done. I know I'm not the only one who has been expected to embark on an insufficiently vetted initiative without the prep time or training necessary to make it a success. Policy enforcement is more likely to be inconsistent when the policy itself is poorly understood.

Here's a quick example to illustrate how a consistent approach to policy enforcement can be a trust pillar. Imagine a school where teachers have identified tardiness as a disruptive problem. Hearing their concerns, the leadership team works over the summer to find a solution. First, they get input from teacher leaders about what will and won't work in terms of a new tardiness policy. They draft and develop a plan. In the days leading up to the first day of school, they design and deliver all-staff training on the expectations, communication, and consequences for students who are tardy. At the beginning-of-year orientation and welcome events, the leadership team communicates the changes clearly and simply with students and parents.

When the new policy is fully implemented, it can be enforced with the full understanding and buy-in of students and staff. Every student—and their parents—will know exactly what will happen if they are late. With no surprise changes and no exceptions, they can trust the fairness of the response.

Handling crises with calm

A principal friend of mine, an energetic gentleman who has endless enthusiasm for his work, shifts into an unexpected gear whenever a crisis arises: he gets more deliberate. Although he is thinking quickly, outwardly he appears to slow down. He uses a low, calming voice. He walks at a purposeful pace. He communicates precisely. When an emergency arises—whether it's a student having a mental health crisis, a safety situation, or a student altercation—students instinctively look for him; they want him there, in the room, bringing his calm authority to the response.

I once worked with a principal navigating the worst of all scenarios, a student's death. Word of the tragic car accident spread quickly during the evening hours and left the school community reeling. This principal sprang into action. She drew up a communication and response plan overnight, then gathered her team before school the next day to refine the plan and assign everyone specific roles and duties. As the school day passed, this principal served as the "command center" for all communication. In the days following the tragedy, she acted as a sort of emotional lighthouse for her school, handling the crisis with grace and excellence and earning the trust of the grieving community.

Showing Students You Are Trust Willing

Students want to be trusted, and they like it when adults recognize that they *can* be trusted. Trusting students has a direct relation to student academic success, too. Research by Goddard and colleagues (2001) conducted with 4th grade students in urban elementary schools found that schools with a high number of teachers who trusted in their students had higher levels of student achievement.

Teacher trust in students improves student achievement.

How can principals demonstrate the trust students are looking for and want to see? Once again, the general approach is to let students step into leadership roles, elevate student voice, and give them chances to show they should be trusted. Here are some more specific approaches.

Prioritize high standards and collective efficacy

As educators, we know students can meet high standards, and as principals who are familiar with research on collective efficiency, we know the transformative power of this knowledge. Indeed, a staff's collective belief in their power to positively educate students is the single biggest indicator of student achievement (Hattie, 2012).

Because principals often interact most with students who are struggling, it can be tempting to listen to voices suggesting that maybe the bar shouldn't be set quite so high. Maybe we shouldn't ask so much or expect so much from our kids. To be trust willing is to insist on the opposite. It's to make sure the entire school keeps expectations high, understands why that matters, and believes in our collective impact.

Show you value student ideas and perspectives

While some of the many ideas students have for how to make school better may not be feasible, making an effort to listen to and treat student ideas seriously reinforces the *open mindset* trust pillar, assuring students that you value them. Collaboration with student leadership groups presents a great opportunity for this work, provided the groups reflect a diversity of students with different perspectives.

A principal I know was approached by a student affinity group advocating the school add a release day for a particular religious holiday. This principal did not have the authority to add an excused day off school and knew this request was a long shot, but he took a few of the group's leaders and their proposal to his supervising council for discussion. After the students shared their proposal—what the holiday was, why it was important, why time off was justified—the principal added compelling remarks about the importance of trusting in the students. "They are the reason we are here," he said. "Surely we can adjust our perspectives to make room for theirs."

After some discussion and a round or two of follow-up questions, the council proposed adjusting their school's policies to allow all students one no-questions-asked release day for religious purposes per year. There was one detractor on the council who was certain students would abuse the new policy by requesting an excused absence for a "skip day." The principal again defended the students. "These young people brought this request with a genuine purpose. They know what they are asking is unique and different, and they are grateful you are opening your minds to a change. In the spirit of that gratitude, I do not anticipate students will abuse this privilege."

The proposal passed in a vote, and in the end, the principal was right. Only on legitimate holy days did students request an excused absence, and it turned out to be a very small number of students utilizing the new protocols. The principal's valuation of the legitimacy of the students' request, along with his help navigating a change in policy, showed his willingness to trust that the students knew what was best for them.

Prioritize home-school partnerships

All principals have students who are navigating complicated in-school challenges as well as complicated home environments. Efforts to make communication and collaboration between school and home as honest and seamless as possible are a powerful investment in these students' success and a very powerful demonstration of trust willingness.

One of the trickiest parts is communicating a student's challenges in a way that does not cause additional stress or problems at home. I have a cousin whose son struggled during his first few years in school. The head of the charter school called my cousin almost daily to outline her son's poor behavior choices and lack of academic progress. Absent significant improvement, the head explained, the school would have no choice but to kick him out. My cousin envisioned her son literally being kicked out of the building and left to stand alone outside. It seemed like they didn't want her son in that school, my distressed cousin told me. They didn't have resources to help him, and they wanted him out.

She withdrew him, enrolled him in another school, and felt the difference immediately. When talking about her son, this school used terms like *we* and *us* to communicate that my cousin was in the conversation and felt part of the team: *We should get together and make a plan to help all of us during his transition period.* This school invited my cousin's child to meet with his new support team and talk about how he felt at school and what triggered his anger. They were intentional in providing a safe, compassionate environment for both the child and the mother. In other words, they were willing to open their dialogue—and their trust—to the boy's mother. Knowing her son extremely well and being in a safe, supportive environment where she wasn't being put in a defensive position, she was able to honestly acknowledge his difficulties and suggest ways he might be helped. The school was open to her suggestions and incorporated them into a positive support plan. In time, the boy settled into a routine and responded well. Both the student and the parent got enormous reassurance from a school being willing to trust in his abilities to acclimate and succeed.

Provide connections to available resources

If a student struggles, schools can capitalize on trusting relationships by offering resources and connections. When a family is in crisis, a school with an established referral process to outside counselors or mental health experts can mobilize solutions more quickly. Some districts have consultation contracts with psychologists, mental health experts, physicians, or parenting experts who can offer parents ideas, suggestions, and insight. When these experts liaise between home and school, a mutually trusting dialogue opens up between adults and students. An example I'd point out is The Hope Squad®, a peer-to-peer suicide prevention program in which specially trained students serve as trusted sources for peers who are struggling and need help.

Trust in what students value

While teachers, principals, and parents may have particular goals and visions for a child's school experience, we should never forget that students have their own ideas about this. Individual priorities and mindsets vary, of course, but in general, students care about being challenged, about being seen, and about fitting in. They also care about lunch. They care about new technology. They care about their friends. They want freedom, study space, independence, and autonomy. Most want to be part of something at school—clubs, sports, performing arts, extracurriculars. Others prioritize their life outside school, filled with friends, hobbies, and in-person and online communities. Some students might care about test scores and class rank; others may not.

I have seen many well-intentioned educators assume students are all the same in their goals and mindsets or, worse, assume students value the same things adults value. By way of example, there has been recent emphasis on directing students toward a career path, sometimes as early as 6th or 7th grade. While I understand the impulse to ensure students have the foundation for their eventual profession, I vehemently disagree with pressuring middle school students to decide on a career based on the results of an aptitude score or two. Adults asking students to be adults before they are ready is a recipe for tension and frustration. It's far better to trust that students have their own timelines, priorities, and interests. That doesn't mean we shouldn't encourage them or push them to push themselves. But we shouldn't push them toward a particular path. Educators' role is to expose students to opportunities to think, grow, and explore, and to remove barriers to these opportunities.

A principal who puts students first—their values but also their hopes, their potential, and their success—is definitely demonstrating trust willingness.

It requires patience and grace to earn student trust and to trust them to give their best effort at school.

Students who trust their principal are more likely to have a stronger identification with their schools, which lowers their risk of emotional or physical withdrawal from school and increases motivation, assignment completion, disruption, truancy, behaviors, delinquency, drug use, school crime, and violence (Mitchell & Forsyth, 2004). Added to a reference we made in Chapter 2 in which Liebowitz and Porter (2019) remind us that there is a direct correlation between principals' trust behaviors and the learning that happens in schools, it is clear that student trust in their principal has an impact on their academic success.

7

Self-Trust and Beyond

Trust with students, parents, and teachers grows though small interactions over time. It is the cumulative effect of countless relational exchanges and dozens of tiny moments.

But what about the small moments we have with ourselves? The conversations we have in our own minds about who we are and what we can accomplish? Many times, principals reflect on decisions they've made, initiatives they've led, and problems they face, and all they can see are their own flaws and faults. This is *leadership insecurity*, a cousin of imposter syndrome. It isn't helpful, and it is all too common.

Consider how athletes, artists, and entertainers are all called to perform under intense pressure. Professionals in these fields are often trained to recognize that the inner workings of their own minds have a profound effect on their results. Sports psychology is a whole field to itself! Venus Williams has spoken about confidence being the thing that makes her a winner. Michael Phelps assures that "with confidence and trust in yourself and those around you, there are no limits" (Phelps & Abrahamson, 2008, p. 6). Vladimir Horowitz, one of the greatest pianists of the 20th century, is quoted as saying, "Without false modesty, I feel that, when I'm on the stage, I'm the king, the boss of the situation" (Po Sim Head, 2020, para. 23).

How do some professionals have such confidence, while others are struck by self-doubt? Why do some principals seem to trust themselves, while others don't—or can't?

Self-Trust 101

The concept of *self-trust* has not yet been covered in this book, but it's time to give it some thought. As school leaders, we're not called on to study self-trust during our training or even consider it, really. So, let's do a little bit of that now.

It's generally assumed that a principal has trust in themselves. At any rate, teachers, students, and parents seem to assume that principals have the answers and *should* be confident. We should know all the right policies, procedures, and protocols to run a school with skill and wisdom. We should have quick and accurate answers to all questions.

But every day, principals face complex issues that are often out of our control. If we falter or handle problems in ways that others don't like, they can get upset and question our leadership. Over time, stress accumulates, and the weight of our responsibilities can get heavier. A friend of mine once said, "The best day to be a principal is the first day," and I laughed out loud when she said it, because it's true. When you're a principal, each new day is another chance to mess up and feel lousy about your mistakes, leading to more insecurities and more self-doubting questions about your ability to make a difference.

The best tool to combat this feeling is inner faith—a commitment to believing in yourself as a leader, staying true to your guiding values, and dedicating time and effort to the work of cultivating self-trust.

Self-Trust and School Culture

A school leader's self-trust is closely connected to the culture of the school they lead. After all, it's easier to be confident in one's leadership when students, teachers, and community members appreciate you, respect one another, and don't view every problem that arises as an indicator of your failure. The two concepts—a trusting school culture and a sense of self-trust—are so intertwined that it's common for leaders to try to build confidence by focusing on and improving overall school culture.

Not long ago, a principal in a popular social media group I belong to asked what she could do to improve her school culture. She was questioning her own ability to lead her school. Morale was low, she said. Parents were distrustful, teachers were resentful, and students were exhibiting behaviors of disrespect and dismissiveness. "What can I do to build trust?" the principal asked. As is typical in online groups made up of thousands of opinionated and anonymous educators, the conversation was not overly helpful. Many criticized the principal—first, for thinking that building trust was her responsibility, and second, for thinking that building trust would change (or fix) anything. Some commenters even got a little combative with one another.

The "why is this your responsibility?" criticism really stuck with me. Who *is* responsible for trust within a school environment and just in general? Who builds trust, who tears it down, and who gets to decide when it's irreparable? Who gets to decide when it's strong? Trust is in the eyes of the beholder, but it's also in the eyes of the participant. Logically, responsibility for trust *can't* belong to one person alone—it *must* be a collective effort. Let me say that again: *Principals, the responsibility for building trust does not fall on you and you alone.* While you have a lot of influence, and while you can do your best to apply concepts in this book, you cannot possibly oversee, manage, or intervene with all the relationships within your school and connected to your school that require trust or are tested by trust. Knowing this is important for your own self-worth and self-actualization as a leader. None of us can do it all. We can't be responsible for everyone else's happiness and satisfaction.

What can we do, then? As discussed in Chapter 2, Patrick Lencioni (2002) believes that trust is rooted in an ability and willingness to be vulnerable with others. As such, principals who value trust can start by demonstrating their own vulnerability. There's no weakness implied here; this kind of vulnerability is about an authentic willingness to take risks, knowing you might lose face. Being vulnerable also means accepting that mistakes and failure are part of the leadership process. It also means encouraging others to take risks and being willing to share some of the work of leadership.

Let others on your team, in your school, and in your life be vulnerable, too. Accept it. Appreciate it. Principals who demonstrate and allow vulnerability grow teams who know how to work through conflict in a healthy way; they also commit to teamwork and shared outcomes, accept accountability, and stay focused on results (Lencioni, 2002).

Doing Your Best

Last December, at a statewide association holiday celebration for administrators, I bumped into a principal I hadn't seen in some time. I was happy to see her! "I feel so behind" I said, as we hugged. "Catch me up. How are you?"

With a wry laugh, she said, "Well, I only cried twice today."

Oh, no, I thought. There was a lot to unpack in that sentence.

We sat down on a few nearby chairs. My principal friend (I'll call her Sarah) needed a listening ear, and I was happy to lend it. As she spoke, I saw that she was struggling under the weight of heavy stress and anxiety. She was questioning everything she did and obsessing about how she could do better. Her school faced a lot of challenges—truancy, apathy, discipline, and lackluster community engagement. But she was making the common mistake I have mentioned. Sarah was assuming these problems were hers and hers alone to solve. In fact, she seemed to think they were all her fault. Even if she hadn't directly caused the attendance, discipline, and morale issues, she hadn't succeeded in fixing them. To her, this felt like just as much of a failure.

Worrying about these problems and her role in them literally kept Sarah up at night, she confessed. Yes, she recognized that her insecurity was feeding on itself and that she was blaming herself excessively, but she didn't know how to pull up from the spiral. "What should I do?" she moaned.

"You need to build your confidence," I said.

This was a terrible response. Telling someone who is losing faith in themselves to "be more confident" or "stop worrying" doesn't help. Gaining confidence isn't a matter of deciding to be more confident, like flipping a switch; it's ongoing work requiring time and patience. Luckily, I recognized my mistake and quickly recalibrated.

"Do you think you are a good leader?" I asked her.

"Well, yes," Sarah said. "In general, I am. But not these days. Not in my school, and not with these students and staff."

"Do you think you are doing your best?"

She thought for a moment before replying. "Yes, I am. But my best is not enough."

This was a worrying conclusion, but I'd heard something I liked. Somewhere deep inside, Sarah did believe in herself and her abilities, but she was covering it up with qualifiers: *I am a good leader, but. . . . I am doing my best, but. . . .* Her words also reminded me of an epiphany I'd had many, many years ago. I was a track athlete, and I was facing one of the biggest races of my life, competing against one of the strongest runners in the state. I spent weeks worrying about it. I studied my rival's stats, compared them against my own, obsessed about possible strategies that might give me an edge. I tossed and turned at night, dreaming about ways I might spectacularly and publicly humiliate myself. But two nights before the race, I had a life-changing epiphany. Its simplicity struck me like a thunderbolt: *All I can do is my best. I will run as fast as I can, and the rest is out of my control.* It is so simple that I almost feel awkward sharing it. Shouldn't this have been something I already knew? Well, of course. In fact, my coaches had been telling me the exact same thing for years. But I'd never truly believed it until . . . well, until I actually believed it. Until I trusted myself that I *would* do my best, that "running as fast as I can" was a goal in itself. Until I accepted that I did not need to be responsible for controlling an entire scenario and outcome, I did not have peace.

This same epiphany can be applied to school leadership. We can work hard, build relationships, read books, put in extra hours, network, and do all the things suggested by our mentors and colleagues. In the end, though, it's still hard work, and we will still have problems.

But if we trust ourselves, knowing we can and will always do our best and that we can control only what is within our control, we will have done good work.

"If you are doing your best, you are... well, doing your best," I said to Sarah. "Your best *has* to be enough. How can you remind yourself of this at the end of each day?"

The answer, of course, is rooted in self-trust. Learning—or remembering—to trust yourself is a uniquely nuanced effort for principals. We have already acknowledged some of the challenges of the position—the need to oversee instruction; to connect with students, even when they are not being their best selves; to manage parent expectations; and to meet all the federal, state, and societal demands placed on schools. Jamie Vollmer (2010) summarized it this way: "Principals are asked to be both efficient branch managers and brilliant instructional leaders; they have become the shock absorbers of the system—squeezed by directives from above and demands from below" (p. 6).

Shock absorbers. This visual feels eerily accurate, in both literal ways (every principal I know has had to intervene in physical altercations between students or between students and staff) and figurative ones. Principals work a job that requires them to manage people and navigate an ever-increasing list of mandates, all within a school calendar that refuses to add time or days and a system that demands long hours and very little return on the time investment (Vollmer, 2010). These challenges are not the fault of students, staff, or parents; they proceed from a faulty system. Blaming people for the outcomes of an inherently flawed system, Vollmer says, is a "terrible mistake that affects politicians, business leaders, academics, bureaucrats, media pundits, and even educators,... [and] misidentifying the core problem has cost America's taxpayers billions of dollars and America's educators untold hours of wasted effort. Most troubling, it has cost millions of America's young people the opportunity to succeed" (p. 6).

Building Self-Trust

Much has been written, debated, and legislated in efforts to improve and reform schools, but there is very little a principal can do when there is a larger system reinforcing the status quo. Fortunately, there are lots of things a principal can do to influence the experiences of students, staff, and families. All that's needed is enough self-trust. Here are some ways to develop more of it.

Present yourself with confidence and humility

When teachers believe that their principals are confident and humble, they rank them as more effective (Oyer, 2015). Principals who are *confident* have reflected on their successes as much as their weaknesses. Principals who are *humble* know they need to keep learning and growing.

I know that *be confident and be humble* is not the most original advice for school leaders, but it's truly among the most valuable. In terms of humility, remember that because you are human, you will make mistakes. To be human is to be imperfect. When reflecting on your professional decisions, your tenure, and your students' outcomes, you will invariably hit on something you wish you'd done differently. Not until you retire or leave the profession altogether will you have days in which you don't want a little bit of a redo! Accepting your imperfection is the essence of humility.

Remember, too, that you were hired to lead your school because someone, or a group of someones, believed in you. They thought you were the best person to lead your building. They trusted your knowledge, your experience, and your skill set. What are the characteristics you carry that might have been most valued by that person or group? Think about the skills you bring to your position. Think about your wisdom, your talent, and your work ethic. Why do those things make you uniquely qualified to do your job well? This is how you maintain your confidence.

Principals who are both confident and humble are more effective leaders.

Prioritize team over self

Ask anyone who has been on a successful athletic team, workplace team, or family team, and they will talk about how being on a strong team builds confidence in every member. It feels good to be part of something with other like-minded, focused people. It's a great feeling to know what one's role is and how combining one's contributions with others' strengths enhances the experience for everyone. Caring about our teammates' successes and celebrating together produces results, and producing results lifts collective and individual confidence.

Practice managing your emotions

When upsetting news comes my way, my initial reaction is often intense anxiety. I feel a physical flush and get jittery. I have learned to see this as a warning: if I don't press pause, there's a risk I will react impulsively and recklessly. With practice and time, I have gotten good at making myself stop, walk away, and wait to respond. I cannot allow my impulsive emotions to take over, because when I am in that state, I have zero perspective. Here's the thing: every time I take a break and wait for my calm and reasonable self to prevail, I wind up feeling more confident in myself and my judgment. *I handled that well,* I can honestly say. Every time I do it, I trust myself more.

Don't rush a solution

Similarly, rushing to solve a problem as quickly as possible usually leads to a less than ideal outcome. Most "crises" we face will be resolved more effectively if we take the time to address them: think, gather feedback, and *then* react. What's more, in many situations, the other people involved might be completely convinced that there is an emergency; it will be up to you, their leader, to remind them that it is not.

I find it comforts others when they come to me, hair on fire, anxious and worried about something that feels really, really big, and I say, "This isn't an emergency. We have time to fix this. We have time to think." When I say those things, I am often met with a relieved exhale. *Oh, OK. It's not an emergency. I am in a room with someone who is calm and assured.*

Assume—and accept—you are missing something

To understand how valuable this mindset is, play it out the other way. A principal who assumes they understand everything is guaranteed to miss something. So ask the questions. What might you be overlooking or misinterpreting? What are the layers of the situation you're facing? What are the details? Who will be affected? How will the process work? What else might you be missing? The neatest trick of assuming you're missing something is that when it proves to be true, your confidence increases. You *knew* you didn't know, because *you're just that good.*

Move toward conflict

Managing conflict is a natural and necessary part of working with people. Ironically, completely avoiding conflict is a way to weaken our relationships. Others lose trust in us, and then we lose trust in ourselves. But if we rely on trust pillars, such as competence, honesty, and professionalism, we will learn the value of leaning into conflict and how to anticipate it, analyze it, and act upon it (Schwanke, 2024). In doing so, those pillars establish us as willing, open, and capable in conflict resolution. Each time we successfully mediate or manage a conflict, we'll feed our skillset and build more self-trust.

Give credit to others

Letting go of the pressure to impress is freeing. The person who stands up and says, "This was a team effort," is also a person who isn't competing for the spotlight.

Part of a principal's job, I think, is to shine the light on others. Principals do not need to make every decision and be at the head of every initiative. Instead, they might facilitate, removing barriers so that others can succeed. Providing support and service to others is a self-trust pillar—much more validating than elbowing someone out of the way to make yourself look good. And thing is, it makes you look good, too. Everyone receiving credit and even those who are hearing about it will know you've played a role as a leader. This knowledge boosts their trust in you.

Be positive

When heading into meetings or events, I try to remind myself to be the most positive person in the room. This mindset determines the tone of many conversations I have, and it often improves the outcome.

Saying things like "Yes, I see your point; let's think about how that might work" rather than "No, that'll never work" opens both possibility and opportunity.

My deliberate optimism doesn't mean that I am blind to problems or use positivity as a tool to cover legitimate negative vibes. I was once accused of "toxic positivity," a hurtful but profound accusation; I still reflect on it. I am careful to avoid glossing over problems, dismissing negativity, or making someone feel "wrong" when they are struggling. Instead, I simply want my positivity to improve someone's outlook, not diminish it. When positive people work together, it seems to increase hope and energy. Sharing that energy is what principals can strive to do for others.

Seek and pay attention to feedback

Not long ago, I was part of a meeting with two colleagues in which I said a few offhand disparaging things about an initiative we were considering. My colleagues expressed concern, but we moved on quickly and I didn't think much about it. Later, I sensed tension in the air and debated whether to address it. When the tension didn't seem to dissipate, I asked them if we could talk. "Give me feedback," I said.

It turned out that my comments had been perceived as offensive and brusque. I was taken aback, but I asked myself to really hear what my colleagues had said. It was a timely reminder that leaders need to pay attention to how our words and actions are interpreted. For us, ongoing reflection on the impact we're having on others is like a chef regularly sharpening her knives. A knife that's not properly cared for will get dull and ineffective, and when you first notice this, the smart thing to do is sharpen the knife. As leaders, we can and will make mistakes. But we must challenge ourselves to pay attention, to notice, and to hone our skills and mindsets accordingly.

Accept compliments

Others will extend compliments, gratitude, and appreciation for your work. Not on a consistent basis, and not always in the ways you expect or wish they would—but the gratitude is there. How will you respond?

As a new school leader, I didn't know what to do in these situations. I wanted to be a "servant leader," and so I felt I didn't deserve gratitude and tended to deflect it. I've changed my mind about that. Serving others doesn't mean I don't get to be appreciated. It doesn't mean I have to ignore or dismiss compliments. On the contrary, I should listen closely, and I should cling to any moment in which other people say they are glad I am their leader.

Be a chameleon

Principals are usually equally adept at talking with 5-year-olds and 85-year-olds. They are accustomed to adjusting their communication approach to the various stakeholders they encounter. A principal needs to know the audience—the style of communication most likely to strike a chord with them, the topics they'll connect with, how receptive or unreceptive they'll be to the message, and so on. In a lot of ways, a principal's work is a nuanced performance.

That doesn't mean "faking it" or not being your authentic self; code switching and shape shifting is not the same as being inauthentic. Sharpening your communication and presentation skills and learning to blend and adapt will build your confidence and boost your sense that you can trust yourself to handle all sorts of situations with all sorts of people.

Get over it

If you've made a mistake or made someone mad or handled something poorly, you have two choices: marinate in it or move on.

I'll share a silly but applicable example of this. I was a new principal leading one of my first department meetings. During the final rotation of an activity that had everyone moving around the room, in an effort to show my energetic personality (and a little sass), I decided to skip to my next station. I tripped on my heel and fell. My skirt flew over my head and, in my scramble to get it back where it belonged, my arms knocked over a portable podium. It crashed to the ground. Everyone turned to look. I was horrified and embarrassed. I flushed red, holding back tears of mortification. I wanted to disappear. I apologized, then apologized again, then tried to make a joke of it, then apologized again.

Finally, a kind teacher reached over and touched my hand. "Let it go," he said. "You're thinking about this far more than anyone else in this room is thinking about it. The more you talk about it, the more it is going to become and remain a thing." I shut up. He was right, too; I'm sure no one else in that room even remembers the incident. I do, and I still blush a little thinking about it, but at that moment, I needed to move on, let it go, and trust that I would overcome it.

This situation applies to any mistake. Acknowledge and apologize, but don't let it define who you are, and certainly don't let it impede your future leadership.

Parting Words

"I hate to ruin the ending for you, but everything is going to be OK." In my office, I keep a giant sign with this message on it. It's a constant and necessary reminder.

The work of a principal is a complicated and ever-changing experience. It's a marathon of sorts, requiring training and pacing. Improvement and confidence are built through practice handling both wins and losses. The goal is to get to a point of the journey in which you *do* believe in yourself, and you *don't* doubt your ability to overcome the next challenge that will invariably come your way.

You will learn to trust yourself. You'll learn, because self-trust is an accumulation of all the other things you get to learn in a day, a year, a career. You'll learn to build and repair trust as you learn more about the people you work with and about yourself, too. If there is one guarantee of the principalship, it's that it will teach you a lot about yourself and force you to learn more each and every day. In the end, trust in others, trust in yourself, and trust in your shared work will all come together and will make for a deeply fulfilling journey.

Acknowledgments

I am deeply grateful for my husband, Jay, and my children, Jackson and Autumn, whose unwavering support and inspiration uplift me every day. Your love and encouragement make all the difference.

A heartfelt thank you to ASCD Books Senior Acquisitions Editor Susan Hills, whose patience and guidance have been instrumental in my writing journey from the very beginning. I am also immensely appreciative of Senior Editor Katie Martin, whose dedication and expertise helped bring the final product to life. To the entire ASCD publications team—including Anthony Rebora, Genny Ostertag, Tara Laskowski, and its many talented artists, editors, and contributors: your commitment to supporting educators worldwide is truly invaluable.

I would also like to express my sincere gratitude to my superintendent, Dr. John Marschhausen; the members of my district's Board of Education; and my incredible colleagues. Your support, collaboration, and passion for education continue to inspire me every day. I am honored to work alongside such dedicated professionals.

References

Barlow, V. (2001). *Trust and the principalship.* Unpublished doctoral dissertation, University of Calgary, Alberta.

Björk, L. G., & Kowalski, T. J. (Eds.). (2005). *The contemporary superintendent: Preparation, practice, and development.* Corwin.

Bloch, R. I., & Karson, M. J. (1972). Comparison data in public sector bargaining. *Journal of Urban Law, 50*, 717.

Blount, J. M. (1998). *Destined to rule the schools: Women and the superintendency, 1873–1995.* SUNY Press.

Bozman, C. E., Sr. (2011). *The effects of principals' leadership styles, teacher efficacy, and teachers' trust in their principals on student achievement.* ProQuest.

Brunner, C., Grogan, M., & Björk, L. (2002). Shifts in the discourse defining the superintendency: Historical and current foundations of the position. In J. Murphy (Ed.), *The educational leadership challenge: Redefining leadership for the 21st century* (pp. 211–238). University of Chicago Press.

Bukko, D., Liu, K., & Johnson, A. H. (2021). Principal practices that build and sustain trust: Recommendations from teachers in a high-trust school. *Planning & Changing, 50*(1), 58–74.

Burke, M. A., & Sass, T. R. (2013). Classroom peer effects and student achievement. *Journal of Labor Economics, 31*(1), 51–82.

Chen, G. (2022, March 7). A history of public schools. *Public School Review.* https://www.publicschoolreview.com/blog/a-history-of-public-schools

Chughtai, A. A., & Buckley, F. (2009). Linking trust in the principal to school outcomes: The mediating role of organizational identification and work engagement. *International Journal of Educational Management, 23*(7), 574–589.

Citrin, J., & Stoker, L. (2018). Political trust in a cynical age. *Annual Review of Political Science, 21*, 49–70.

Conant, J. B. (1959). *The American high school today: A first report to interested citizens.* McGraw-Hill.

Conway, M. (2013, August 8). *A study of American high school contributions to the world wars, 1917–1949*. Primary Research. https://primaryresearch.org/a-study-of-american-high-school-contributions-to-the-world-wars-1917-1949/

Dotson, J. (n.d.). *The early United States land system*. Washington Map Society. https://washmapsociety.wildapricot.org/resources/Documents/Articles%20and%20Papers%20Page/Explore%20-%20Articles%20-%20Early%20US%20Land%20System.pdf

Durham, J. T. (1959). The Conant report: A critique. *The Clearing House, 34*(3), 177–181. http://www.jstor.org/stable/30193407

Edwards, M. E. (2006). *The modern school superintendent: An overview of the role and responsibilities in the 21st century*. iUniverse.

Fowler, F. C. (2013). *Policy studies for educational leaders: An introduction*. Allyn & Bacon Educational Leadership Series. Pearson.

Francis, G. L., Blue-Banning, M., Haines, S. J., Turnbull, A. P., & Gross, J. M. (2016a). Building "our school": Parental perspectives for building trusting family-professional partnerships. *Preventing School Failure: Alternative Education for Children and Youth, 60*(4), 329–336.

Francis, G. L., Blue-Banning, M., Turnbull, A. P., Hill, C., Haines, S. J., & Gross, J. M. (2016b, September). Culture in inclusive schools: Parental perspectives on trusting family-professional partnerships. *Education and Training in Autism and Developmental Disabilities, 51*(3), 281–293.

Fultz, M. (2004). The displacement of Black educators post-*Brown*: An overview and analysis. *History of Education Quarterly, 44*(1), 11–45.

Ganzel, B., & Reinhardt, C. (2003). *School Days*. Wessels Living History Farm. https://livinghistoryfarm.org/farming-in-the-1930s/

George, C. E., Ingle, W. K., & Pogodzinski, B. (2018). Exploring the politics of collective bargaining and unions in education. *Educational Policy, 32*(2), 1–9. https://doi.org/10.1177/0895904817752882

Glass, T. E., & Franceschini, L. A. (2007). *The state of the American school superintendency: A mid-decade study*. Rowman & Littlefield.

Goddard, R. D., Tschannen-Moran, M., & Hoy, W. K. (2001). A multilevel examination of the distribution and effects of teacher trust in students and parents in urban elementary schools. *Elementary School Journal, 102*(1), 3–17.

Gordon, M. F., & Louis, K. S. (2009). Linking parent and community involvement with student achievement: Comparing principal and teacher perceptions of stakeholder influence. *American Journal of Education, 116*(1), 1–31.

Gregory, A., & Ripski, M. B. (2008). Adolescent trust in teachers: Implications for behavior in the high school classroom. *School Psychology Review, 37*(3), 337–353.

Hannaway, J., & Mittleman, J. (2011). Education politics and policy in an era of evidence. In D. E. Mitchell & R. L. Crowson (Eds.), *Shaping education Policy* (pp. 97–107). Routledge.

Harvey, T. R., & Drolet, B. (2004). *Building teams, building people: Expanding the fifth resource.* R&L Education.

Hattie, J. (2012). *Visible learning for teachers: Maximizing impact on learning.* Routledge.

Hayes, S. C. (2005). *Get out of your mind and into your life: The new acceptance and commitment therapy.* New Harbinger.

Hayes, S. C. (2020). *A liberated mind: How to pivot toward what matters.* Penguin.

History.com Editors. (2009, November 9). Columbine shooting. *History.com.* https://www.history.com/topics/1990s/columbine-high-school-shootings.

Hoy, W. K., & Tschannen-Moran, M. (1999). Five faces of trust: An empirical confirmation in urban elementary schools. *Journal of School Leadership, 9*(3), 184–208. https://doi.org/10.1177/105268469900900301

Hunt, S. L., & Staton, A. Q. (1996). The communication of educational reform: A nation at risk. *Communication Education, 45*(4), 271–292. https://doi.org/10.1080/03634529609379058

International Task Force on Teachers for Education 2030. (2019). Teacher data: SDG indicators and other sources. https://teachertaskforce.org/what-we-do/Knowledge-production-and-dissemination/data-teachers

Kirst, M. W. (1994, January). A changing context means school board reform. *Phi Delta Kappan, 75*(5), 378–379.

Knepper, G. W. (2002). *The official Ohio lands book.* Auditor of State.

Knezevich, S. J. (1984). *Administration of public education* (4th ed.). Harper & Row.

Koerner, J. D. (1960). The tragedy of the Conant Report: A "personal testament." *Phi Delta Kappan, 42*(3), 121–124. http://www.jstor.org/stable/20342526

Kowalski, T. J. (2003). *Responses to student needs and public dissatisfaction in contemporary school administration.* Allyn & Bacon.

Kowalski, T. J. (2005). Evolution of the school district superintendent position. In L. G. Björk & T. Kowalski (Eds.), *The contemporary superintendent: Preparation, practice, and development* (pp. 1–18). Corwin.

Kutsyuruba, B., Walker, K. D., & Noonan, B. (2010). The ecology of trust in the principalship. *Journal of Educational Administration and Foundations, 21*(1), 23–47.

Lake, B. J., Billingsley, B., & Stewart, A. (2018). Building trust and responding to parent-school conflict. In J. B. Crockett, B. Billingsley, & M. L.

Boscardin (Eds.), *Handbook of leadership and administration for special education*, (2nd ed., pp. 265–278). Routledge.

Lencioni, P. (2002). *The five dysfunctions of a team: A leadership fable*. Jossey-Bass.

Lepore, J. (2022, March 14). Wars still rage. *The New Yorker*. https://www.newyorker.com/magazine/2022/03/21/why-the-school-wars-still-rage

Liebowitz, D. D., & Porter, L. (2019). The effect of principal behaviors on student, teacher, and school outcomes: A systematic review and meta-analysis of the empirical literature. *Review of Educational Research, 89*(5), 785–827.

Lutz, M. (2017). The hidden cost of *Brown v. Board*: African American educators' resistance to desegregating schools. *Online Journal of Rural Research & Policy, 12*(4). https://newprairiepress.org/ojrrp/vol12/iss4/2/

Maister, D. H., Green, C. H., & Galford, R. M. (2001). *The trusted advisor*. Touchstone.

Maxwell, W. H. (1904). Superintendent as a man of affairs. *Journal of Education, 59*(10), 147–149.

McArdle, E. (2014). What happened to the Common Core? *Harvard Education Magazine*. https://www.gse.harvard.edu/news/ed/14/09/what-happened-common-core

Mitchell, R. M., & Forsyth, P. B. (2004, November). *Trust, the principal and student identification*. Paper presented at the annual meeting of the University Council for Education Administration, Kansas City, MO.

Moneva, J., & Tribunalo, S. M. (2020). Students' level of self-confidence and performance tasks. *Asia Pacific Journal of Academic Research in Social Sciences, 5*(1), 42–48.

National Commission on Excellence in Education. (1983). *A nation at risk: The imperative for educational reform: A report to the Nation and the Secretary of Education, United States Department of Education*. Author.

Oyer, B. J. (2015). Teacher perceptions of principals' confidence, humility, and effectiveness: Implications for educational leadership. *Journal of School Leadership, 25*(4), 684–719.

Phelps, M., & Abrahamson, A. (2008). *No limits: The will to succeed*. Simon & Schuster.

Po Sim Head, F. (2020, August 22). *20 heartfelt quotes from 20 great pianists*. https://interlude.hk/20-quotes-from-20th-century-pianists/

Price, H. E. (2015). Principals' social interactions with teachers: How principal–teacher social relations correlate with teachers' perceptions of student engagement. *Journal of Educational Administration, 53*(1), 116–139.

Rousmaniere, K. (2013). *The principal's office: A social history of the American school principal.* SUNY Press.

Sass, E. (2021). *American educational history: A hypertext timeline.* https://www.eds-resources.com/educationhistorytimeline.html

Schwanke, J. (2024). *The principal's guide to conflict management.* ASCD.

Simmons, J. C. (2005). Superintendents of color. In L. G. Björk & T. Kowalski (Eds.), *The contemporary superintendent: Preparation, practice, and development* (pp. 251–259). Corwin.

Sinek, S. (2021). *Trust is like love. Both parties have to feel it before it really exists* [Post]. LinkedIn. https://www.linkedin.com/posts/simonsinek_trust-is-like-love-both-parties-have-to-activity-6746992906520805376-

Tschannen-Moran, M., & Gareis, C. R. (2015). Faculty trust in the principal: An essential ingredient in high-performing schools. *Journal of Educational Administration, 53*(1), 66–92.

Tschannen-Moran, M., & Hoy, W. (1998). Trust in schools: A conceptual and empirical analysis. *Journal of Educational Administration, 36*(4), 334–352.

Tuttle, W. M., Jr. (1993). *"Daddy's gone to war": The Second World War in the lives of America's children.* Oxford University Press.

Tyack, D., & Hansot, E. (1982). *Managers of virtue: Public school leadership in America, 1820–1980.* Basic Books.

Tyack, D., Lowe, R., & Hansot, E. (1984). *Public schools in hard times: The Great Depression and recent years.* Harvard University Press.

Verdugo, R. R. (2018). *American education and the demography of the U.S. student population, 1880–2014.* Springer.

Vollmer, J. (2010). *Schools cannot do it alone: Building public support for America's public schools.* Enlightenment Press.

Willie, C. V. (2000). Confidence, trust and respect: The preeminent goals of educational reform. *Journal of Negro Education, 69*(4), 255–262.

Index

accountability, trust pillar of, 107
achievement, 105–106, 132
answers, choosing delayed truth over instant, 58
appearance, killing trust with an undisciplined, 102
auditor, having an, 83–84
authenticity, trust pillar of, 126–127
availability, trust pillar of, 78, 80, 124, 127
award programs, 123–124

behavior, killing trust with undisciplined, 102
benevolence, trust pillar of, 50–51, 84
Bilingual Education Act, 15
Brown v. Board of Education, 10–11

chameleon, building self-trust by being a, 147
circle of trust, 34–35
civil rights movement, 10–11
clarity, trust pillar of, 74–75, 101–102
close-mindedness, a trust killer, 60
collaboration
    to build trust, 51
    to show trust willingness, 91–92
collective bargaining, 11–13
commitment
    killing trust with a lack of, 77–78
    trust pillar of, 126

Common Core State Standards, 16
common school movement, 4–5, 30
communication, components of building trust
    archiving for easy access, 108
    clarity, 129–130
    empathy balanced with professionalism, 111
    end conversations with nowhere to go, 58
    hard conversations, managing with tact and calm, 109–111
    honesty, 129–130
    lookout for conversation stoppers, 110–111
    mass communications on a predictable schedule, 108
    with parents, 107–110
    power dynamics and bias recognized, 110
    remembering the intended outcome, 110
    with students, 108
    tailoring, 108–109
    training and empowering staff, 107
    welcome conversations, 60
communications
    recording, 118–119
    safety planning, 101–102
    trust killers, 102
community, attacks on schools and teachers, 2–4

community-school trust, 8, 10, 13–15
competence, trust pillar of, 53–56, 78, 85, 101, 124
compliments, accepting to build self-trust, 146–147
confident, building self-trust by appearing, 143
confidentiality, 58, 77, 88–89
conflict, building self-trust by moving toward, 145
courage, killing trust with a lack of, 76
crediting others, building self-trust by, 145
crises, handling with calm, 132
culture of trust, 22–24

deception, a trust killer, 59, 77
decisions, killing trust with ambiguous or arbitrary, 123
defensiveness, a trust killer, 104
delegate
    to build trust, 52
    to show trust willingness, 91
desegregation, 10–12
discipline
    trust killers in, 103, 105, 122–123
    trust pillar of consistency in, 130–131
disrespect, a trust killer, 124
distrust
    mistrust vs., 30–31
    training principals in, 32–33, 47–48

education history, United States
    1600s–2020s: timeline of initiatives, 18–20*f*
    1600s: beginnings, 4, 30
    1800s: common schools, 4–5, 30
    1900–1920: politicized school boards, 5–7
    1900–1920: social, wealth, and resource disparities, 5–8

education history, United States (*continued*)
    1914–1918: World War I changes, 7
    1920–1940: enrollment growth, curricular shifts, financial impacts, politicization, community connections, 7–9
    1929–1939: Great Depression, 8–9
    1930–1980: school consolidation, collective bargaining, 11–13
    1940–1960: social tensions, wealth discrepancies, 9–14
    1941–1945: World War II, 9
    1954: desegregation, 10–12
    1970s: crises of leadership, 13–14
    1980–2000: criticism and scrutiny, 14–15
    2000–2024: standardized testing, government mandates, recession, school shootings, pandemic protocols, social tensions, 15–17
    distrust of leadership in, 30, 95
Elementary and Secondary Education Act, 12, 15
embarrassment, killing trust with public, 122
emotional regulation
    to build self-trust, 144
    trust pillar of, 89–90
empathy, balancing with professionalism, 111
engagement, trust pillar of sincere, 109, 127–128
equitable treatment, to build trust, 62–63
exclusivity, a trust killer, 123–124
expertise
    outsourcing as a trust killer, 79, 85
    yielding to greater, 91

favoritism, a trust killer, 61–63, 75–76, 122
feedback
    building self-trust with, 146
    killing trust by refusing, 78
field trips, participating in, 128
forgiveness, 43–44

get over it to build self-trust, 147–148
Goss v. Lopez, 14
government mandates in education, 15–17
Great Depression, 8–9

help, asking for, 84–85
home-school partnerships in trust willingness, 134–135
honesty, trust pillar of, 56–59, 77
humility, building self-trust with, 143

if you don't know, say so to build trust, 57
improvement, trust pillar of committing to, 83
incompetence, a trust killer, 56
Individuals with Disabilities Improvement Act (IDEA), 15
information sharing to build trust, 57–58
initiatives, killing trust with too many new, 75
instructional expectations, killing trust with unclear or uninformed, 74–75

judgments, a trust killer, 51

leaders, components of trusted, 51, 53, 56, 59, 60, 63
leadership, encouraging in
    parents, 37–38
    students, 40–41
    teachers, 36
leadership insecurity, 137
listening, a trust pillar, 86–87, 106–107

mentoring, to show trust willingness, 90–91
micromanaging, avoiding to show trust willingness, 90
mindset, trust pillar of open, 59–60
mistakes, 43–44, 80–83
mistrust, distrust vs., 30–31
modeling trustworthiness and trust willingness, 42

A Nation at Risk: The Imperative for Educational Reform, 14
No Child Left Behind (NCLB) Act, 15
norms, seeking consistent and clear alignment of, 85–86

open-mindedness, trust pillar of, 78, 133
outsourcing expertise, a trust killer, 79, 85
overstepping, a trust killer, 124–125

pandemic protocols, 15–17
parent-principal relationship, achievement and, 105–106
parents
    building trust through communication, 108–110
    distrust of schools and teachers, reasons for, 30, 95
    leadership by, encouraging, 37–38
    principal's trustworthiness, factors in, 31
    schools/teachers, attacks on, 1–4
    voices, elevating, 38–39
    when pushback gets personal, 97–100
    who break trust, 39–40
parents, demonstrating trust willingness to
    elevate their voices, 38–39
    empowering parent leadership, 112–113
    giving them chances, 39–40

parents, demonstrating trust
   willingness to *(continued)*
      identifying key
         communicators, 113
      letting them lead, 37–38
      prioritize the parent-teacher
         relationship, 112
      by social media, 114
parents, trust killers for
   adopting a victim mentality,
      104
   defensiveness, 104
   devaluing parent priorities,
      103
   dismissing safety concerns,
      101–102
   inconsistent student
      discipline, 103
   limiting parent access, 104
   passing the disciplinary buck,
      105
   undisciplined behavior and
      appearance, 102
   weak communication, 102
parents, trust pillars for
   being present and engaged at
      school events, 109
   being responsive and
      accountable, 107
   engaging in frequent, relevant
      communication, 107–109
   following through, 109
   hearing what's being said,
      106–107
   learning and honoring each
      student's story, 111–112
   managing hard conversations
      with tact and calm, 109–111
parent-school partnerships, 96–97,
   134–135
parent-teacher relationship, 112
play, trust pillar of, 129
policy enforcement, trust pillar of
   consistency in, 131
positivity in building self-trust,
   145–146

principal-parent relationship,
   achievement and, 105–106
principals
   1900–1920: responsibilities
      and pressure from school
      boards, 6
   primary purpose of, 29
   training in distrust, 32–33,
      47–48
   trust behaviors-student
      outcomes correlation, 29,
      46
   trustworthiness, factors of, 31
   visualizing a culture of trust,
      23
prioritize to build trust, 52
professionalism, trust pillar of, 61–
   63, 76–77, 78, 101, 104, 127

questions, building trust with, 50–51
quick fixes, killing trust by relying
   on, 78–79

relationships, leveraging to promote
   trustworthiness and trust
   willingness, 43
reliability, trust pillar of, 51–53, 78
resistance, expecting, 90
resources, provide connections to
   available, 135
responsiveness, trust pillar of, 107
rigidity, a trust killer, 60
rules, checking before committing to
   action, 80–81
running away, building trust by not,
   49

safety concerns, killing trust by
   dismissing, 101–102
school-community trust, 8, 10, 13–15
school consolidations, historically,
   11–13
school culture, self-trust and,
   138–140
school-home partnerships,
   characteristics of positive, 96–97

schools
    attacks on, 1–4
    trust divide within, 25–27
school shootings, 15–17
school-society trust, 9
secretiveness, a trust killer, 59
self-promotion, a trust killer, 76–77
self-trust
    concept, 138
    doing your best, 140–142
    everything is going to be OK, 148
    school culture and, 138–140
self-trust, building by
    accepting compliments, 146–147
    assuming-and accepting-you are missing something, 144–145
    being a chameleon, 147
    crediting others, 145
    emotional management, 144
    feedback, 146
    getting over it, 147–148
    moving toward conflict, 145
    not rushing a solution, 144
    positivity, 145–146
    presenting yourself with confidence and humility, 143
    prioritize team over self, 143–144
slowing down, trust pillar of, 79–80
social media, use of, 114
society-school trust, 9
solutions, delaying, 49, 52–53, 58, 144
spite, a trust killer, 51
standardized testing, 15–17
students
    elevate their voices, 41
    fractured trust scenario, 117–120
    freedom of speech, 13–14
    getting to know, 108, 111–112

students (*continued*)
    leadership by, encouraging, 40–41
    principal's trustworthiness, factors in, 31
    visualizing a culture of trust, 24
    who break trust, 41–42
students, demonstrating trust willingness to
    achievement and, 132
    by elevating their voices, 41
    giving them chances, 41–42
    high standards and collective efficacy prioritized, 133
    home-school partnerships, 134–135
    letting them lead, 40–41
    providing connections to available resources, 135
    trust in what they value, 135–136
    valuing student ideas and perspectives, 133–134
students, trust killers for
    ambiguous or arbitrary decisions, 123
    disrespect, 124
    examples of, 120–122
    exclusivity, 123–124
    favoritism, 122
    lack of due process, 122–123
    overstepping, 124–125
    public embarrassment, 122
students, trust pillars for
    authenticity, 126–127
    clear and honest communications, 129–130
    consistency in discipline, 130–131
    consistency in policy enforcement, 131
    crises handled calmly, 132
    engagement, 127–129
    play, 129
    showing commitment, 126
system health aspect of trust, 67–69

teachers
- attacks on, 1–4
- barriers faced by, 66–67
- leadership by, encouraging, 36
- non-educators, frustrations with, 25–27
- number of globally, 22
- reactive mode, 25
- trust in, 22
- visualizing a culture of trust, 23–24
- voices, elevating, 36–37
- who break trust, 37

teachers, demonstrating trust willingness to
- avoid micromanaging, 90
- delegate, 91
- elevate their voices, 36–37
- factors in, 31
- giving them chances, 36–37
- let them lead, 36
- mentor and support, 90–91
- reinforce work collaboratively, 91–92
- yield to greater expertise, 91

teachers, trust killers for
- breaking confidences, 77
- deception, 77
- favoritism, 61–63, 75–76
- lack of commitment, 77–78
- lack of courage, 76
- refusing feedback, 78
- relying on quick fixes, 78–79
- self-promotion, 76–77
- too many new initiatives, 75
- unclear or uninformed instructional expectations, 74–75

teachers, trust pillars for
- acknowledging mistakes, 81–83
- asking for help, 84–85
- being open to listening, 86–87
- checking the rules before committing to action, 80–81

teachers, trust pillars for (*continued*)
- committing to improvement, 83
- confidentiality, 88–89
- emotional regulation, 89–90
- expecting resistance, showing persistence, 90
- having an auditor, 83–84
- honoring the teaching profession, 87–88
- seeing the various sides, 84
- seeking consistent and clear alignment of norms, 85–86
- slowing down, 79–80

teachers-principal compromised trust scenario, 70–74

teaching profession, trust pillar of honoring the, 87–88

teams
- prioritizing to build self-trust, 143–144
- relying on to build trust, 48
- trust in effective, 28

Tinker v. Des Moines Independent School District, 14

training, 107

trust
- broken, 37, 39–42, 44, 46, 70–74
- building, image of, 44–46
- community-school, 8, 10, 13–15
- defining, 21–23
- faces of, 46–47
- reciprocal, 44
- reciprocity of, 27–28
- responsibility for, 139
- in schools, importance of, 29
- societal-school, 9
- vulnerability and, 139–140
- workplace, 27–28

trust, building by. *See also* communication, components of building trust; parents, trust pillars for; students, trust pillars for; teachers, trust pillars for

trust, building by (*continued*)
    admitting uncertainty, 48
    asking more questions, 50–51
    choosing delayed truth over instant answers, 58
    connecting with principal colleagues, 63
    considering the impossible, 60
    delegating, 52
    ending conversations with nowhere to go, 58
    focusing on equitable treatment, 62–63
    honoring confidentiality, 58
    if you don't know, say so, 57
    looking for other answers, 52–53
    not hoarding information, 57–58
    not running away, 49
    pausing to recalibrate, 49
    prioritizing, 52
    relying on a team, 48
    review, reflect, and examine, 55
    starting with yes, 60
    welcoming conversation, 60
    working collaboratively, 51
trust divide, 25–27
trust killers. *See also* parents, trust killers for; students, trust killers for; teachers, trust killers for
    close-mindedness, 60
    deception, 59
    examples of, 46
    incompetence, 56
    leadership approaches, 67–69
    negative judgments, 51
    outsourcing expertise, 79, 85
    refusal to show vulnerability, 49
    rigidity, 60
    secretiveness, 59
    spite, 51
    unkindness, 51

trust killers (*continued*)
    unprofessionalism, 63
    unreliability, 53
trust pillars. *See also* parents, trust pillars for; students, trust pillars for; teachers, trust pillars for
    availability, 78, 80, 124, 127
    benevolence, 50–51, 84
    clarity, 74–75, 101–102
    competence, 53–56, 78, 85, 101, 124
    honesty, 56–59, 77
    image of, 44
    open-mindedness, 59–60, 78, 133
    professionalism, 61–63, 76–77, 78, 101, 104, 127
    reliability, 51–53, 78
    visibility, 80
    vulnerability, 47–49, 80
trust willingness. *See also* parents, demonstrating trust willingness to; students, demonstrating trust willingness to; teachers, demonstrating trust willingness to
    component of, 29
    continuing a circle of trust through, 34–35
    demonstrating, 36–42
    difficulty of, 32–33
    forgiveness and, 43–44
    leveraging relationships to promote, 43
    modeling, 42
    reasons for, 33–35
trustworthiness
    component of, 29–32
    forgiveness and, 43–44
    leveraging relationships to promote, 43
    modeling, 42

uncertainty, building trust by admitting, 48
unkindness, a trust killer, 51

unprofessionalism, a trust killer, 63
unreliability, a trust killer, 53

victim mentality, a trust killer, 104
visibility, trust pillar of, 80
voices, elevating
    parents, 38–39
    students, 41
    teachers, 36–37
volunteering, a trust pillar for students, 129

vulnerability
    trust and, 28, 139–140
    trust pillar of, 47–49, 80

wealth discrepancies, effect in education history, 5–8, 9–14
World War I, 7
World War II, 9

yes, building trust with, 60

About the Author

Jen Schwanke, EdD, has been an educator for almost three decades, teaching or leading at all levels. She is the author of four previous ASCD books and has written hundreds of articles for various education publications. In addition to providing professional development to districts in the areas of school climate, personnel, and instructional leadership, Schwanke presents at conferences for ISTE+ASCD, NAESP, NASSP, AASA, and various state and national education organizations. She is the co-host of the popular *Principal Matters* podcast and an instructor in educational administration at The Ohio State University. Schwanke currently serves as a deputy superintendent in Ohio.

Related ASCD Resources

At the time of publication, the following resources were available (ASCD stock numbers in parentheses).

Am I Cut Out for This? An Educational Leader's Guide to Navigating Self-Doubt by Elizabeth Dampf (#125007)

Embracing MESSY Leadership: How the Experience of 20,000 School Leaders Can Transform You and Your School by Alyssa Gallagher and Rosie Connor (#124011)

The EQ Way: How Emotionally Intelligent School Leaders Navigate Turbulent Times by Ignacio Lopez (#123046)

Finding Your Leadership Soul: What Our Students Can Teach Us About Love, Care, and Vulnerability by Carlos R. Moreno (#123025)

The Principal Reboot: 8 Ways to Revitalize Your School Leadership by Jen Schwanke (#121005)

The Teacher's Principal: How School Leaders Can Support and Motivate Their Teachers by Jen Schwanke (#122035)

You're the Principal! Now What? Strategies and Solutions for New School Leaders by Jen Schwanke (#117003)

What If I'm Wrong? And Other Key Questions for Decisive School Leadership by Simon Rodberg (#121009)

What Can I Take Off Your Plate? A Structural—and Sustainable—Approach to Countering Teacher Burnout by Jill Handley and Lara Donnelly (#125002)

What's Your Leadership Story? A School Leader's Guide to Aligning How You Lead with Who You Are by Gretchen Oltman and Vicki Bautista (#121020)

For up-to-date information about ASCD resources, go to www.ascd.org. You can search the complete archives of *Educational Leadership* at www.ascd.org/el. To contact us, send an email to member@ascd.org or call 1-800-933-2723 or 703-578-9600.

iste+ascd

Transform Instruction to
Transform Students' Lives

Our Transformational Learning Principles (TLPs) are evidence-based practices that ensure students have access to high-impact, joyful learning experiences.

Endorsed by AASA and NASSP, the TLPs provide a shared language and a framework for reimagining teaching and learning, focusing on nurturing student growth, guiding intellectual curiosity, and empowering learners to take ownership of their education.

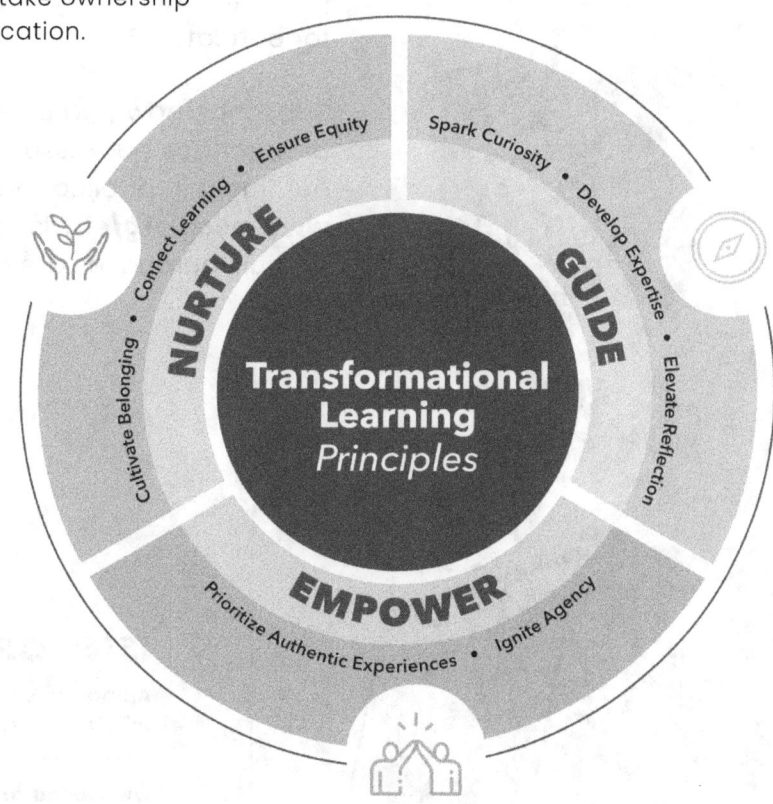

Learn more at **ascd.org/tlps**

DON'T MISS A SINGLE ISSUE OF THIS AWARD-WINNING MAGAZINE.

iste+ascd
educational leadership

If you belong to a Professional Learning Community, you may be looking for a way to get your fellow educators' minds around a complex topic. Why not delve into a relevant theme issue of *Educational Leadership*, the journal written by educators for educators?

Subscribe now and browse or purchase back issues of our flagship publication at **www.ascd.org/el**. Discounts on bulk purchases are available.

iste+ascd

Arlington, VA USA
1-800-933-2723

www.ascd.org
www.iste.org